POP SCARS

POP SCARS

A MEMOIR ON FAME, ADDICTION AND THE DARK SIDE OF 90s POP

Anthony Kavanagh

bl!nk

First published in the UK in 2025 by Blink Publishing
An imprint of Bonnier Books UK
5th Floor, HYLO, 105 Bunhill Row,
London, EC1Y 8LZ

A CIP catalogue record for this book is available from the British Library.

Hardback ISBN: 9781785123122

Also available as an ebook and an audiobook

1 3 5 7 9 10 8 6 4 2

Design and Typeset by Envy Design Ltd
Printed and bound in Great Britain by Clays Ltd, Elcograf S.p.A.

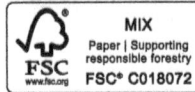

The authorised representative in the EEA is
Bonnier Books UK (Ireland) Limited.
Registered office address: Floor 3, Block 3, Miesian Plaza,
Dublin 2, D02 Y754, Ireland
compliance@bonnierbooks.ie

www.bonnierbooks.co.uk

For the outsiders

CONTENTS

PROLOGUE

A Hollywood ending

It is cold. I am cold. I'm hungover and my head is pounding, and I am thirstier than I have ever been in my life. I am not at my sublet apartment in West Hollywood, nor do I recognise this house I have woken up in; or more to the point, come to in. I'm lying on what feels like a leather sofa, the skin from my elbows sticks to it as I peel myself off. There is not much light except for one perfect stream of Californian sun, which shines directly onto an old framed movie poster of Marlene Dietrich. Her face is illuminated on the wall above me, like a heavenly being, a true icon in all her glory. I pause in a moment of calm and think of that Suzanne Vega song my best friend Andrew used to play me on his Walkman as a kid. All this time and I never realised what it was about.

Marlene on the wall.

I notice my fingernails are black, like I've fallen in

mud or dirt, and there's a small bruise on my arm. I must have fallen over. It won't be the first time, but it's the not remembering that's happening more these days. Stupid vodka. I should stick to beer but it's not very LA. Neither is a beer belly. No casting director wants to see that in this town. I think it's morning but I can't be sure. I reach for my phone, which is next to my head on what feels like a damp cushion with a silky cover on it. I realise it is damp because my hair is wet from sweat, alcohol and God knows what other toxins that are seeping out of me. I can feel my phone screen is cracked but it switches on and I wait with dread for it to start pinging with some evidence of what happened last night, and, more importantly, inform me of where I am. There are empty bottles of Grey Goose and full ashtrays of Marlboro Light dimps on the art deco-looking glass table. Is that what I think it is? It can't be. Surely not. It is. It's a Golden Globe. A real Golden Globe award staring right at me, there in all its glory in pride of place on a book cabinet. Jesus. I squint to read what it says but I can't make it out. My cell phone pings. That all-too-familiar fear and dread arrives. I have six missed calls and twelve new text messages. That's a lot even for me. I can't dare to look. I see crumbs of white powder and a black American Express card lying next to empty plastic wraps on a desk. I get a flashback of being at a bar, Numbers on Santa Monica Boulevard, where I once overheard the gossipy drag queen who DJs at The Abbey tell a punter it was where 'all the male hookers go'. What was I doing there? Who was I with? I then remember talking to an older guy with white hair and thinking he looked like Colonel Sanders. I got in his car with him, it was old-fashioned-looking and bright turquoise, a Chevrolet he said, and we drove down Sunset Strip with Neil Sedaka's greatest hits CD blaring out of the speakers. It's starting to come back to me now.

Oh, Carol.

Oh, fuck, more like.

I can also feel something in my pocket. It feels like a bundle of money, but my skinny jeans are so tight I have to lift myself up to squeeze my hand in. I pull out a scrunched-up dollar bill. No, wait, it's a hundred-dollar bill. Then a fifty and another hundred. Then it hits me. I think I had sex with him. For money.

INTRODUCTION

My mum and dad married in Manchester in a Catholic church, and not long after had a baby that wasn't me. It was my sister Angela, and they all lived as best they could with what they had, somewhat happily, until almost two decades later my mum fell pregnant for the second time after her self-diagnosed stomach ulcer instead turned out to be a baby – me! My dad was from Dublin and my mum was . . .

OK, STOP.

Nobody wants to hear about my childhood. Let's get that fact out of the way first. I wouldn't do that to you, the one who's actually taking the time to read this book, for which I appreciate you doing so, considering this time a few years ago I was purchasing cheap vodka for breakfast to stop the shakes along with a tin of cat food for a cat I didn't have so the shopkeeper thought I was normal. Never mind writing a book. Oh yes, I know you came here for the gritty stuff. That's absolutely fine, in fact, it's a *good* thing. Mainly because what happened to me from the age of 16 onwards had such a dramatic effect on me and who I would become, and then, er, not become, that most of my childhood is a bit of a blur.

I'm not sure I'd want to read a book that's going to witter on about someone's mother being a fortune teller as a child, or how poor they were, or what grades they got (three GCSEs and a U in maths), so why would I put you through that? (Oops, sorry – I just did.)

So don't worry. I'm going to skip the early stuff.

So, let's begin at the proper start, or at least for me when my real life, the one I'd spent every waking hour dreaming of happening, really did actually begin . . .

* * *

I'm going to be a pop star. I'm going to be on the cover of *Smash Hits*. I will be on *Top of the Pops* and win awards. I will move to Hollywood where I will become an actor and create music with the greats, and one day I'll even write a book like all great superstars do.

I will be happy.

Thank you, my gracious and beloved St Anthony, not only my namesake but patron saint of lost causes such as I, for helping me find these precious gifts and for hearing my prayer.

Amen

PS. Just the pop star bit is fine for now

x

FACTORY SETTINGS

It's the summer of 1994, I'm 16 years old, have just left school, and I've been working part-time at McDonald's. Not because I have a burning desire to one day be area manager, but because hair gel, Benson & Hedges cigarettes, pop magazines and CDs won't pay for themselves while I follow my dream of becoming a superstar. The only exciting thing on the horizon at this point is earning my first gold star, but that dream ended when I was caught stealing a Filet-O-Fish and was sacked on the spot. Why such extravagant statements of future success, you may ask? Well, without sounding like a cocky ambitious wannabe, I simply knew that this was going, or more to the point *had*, to happen. I could feel it deep within my being. Call it a premonition, call it absolute delusion, but even in the face of overwhelming evidence of the contrary, I, Anthony Gerard Kavanagh am going to be famous and was willing to walk through a brick wall to make it happen . . .

September, 1994

'Let's try one more club and if we can't get in that one, we're going to McDonald's,' my best mate Andrew says, regarding the now third nightclub we have tried to get in and been refused entry due to looking too young.

'We can't go McDonald's, I've just been fired, remember?' Andrew seems to have forgotten the small detail of my sacking two weeks ago over a shambolic incident with the till at lunchtime and the stolen Filet-O-Fish, with me being the common denominator in both.

'Let's see if we can get in one more then we give up and get a kebab, eh?' says my cousin Sean, who has joined us for tonight's outing after I declared that I wanted to go to a proper nightclub this weekend rather than just the usual pub crawl. So far we have tried a dingy-looking establishment round the back of Oldham Street, where the bouncer took one look at us and said, 'You're joking, aren't you?' and the second one was a slightly more sophisticated place called Lammaars, owned by the beloved and famous drag queen of Manchester Foo Foo Lammar whose much more empathetic bouncer took one look at me and Andrew and said, 'Come back when you're out of your nappies, cock.'

Now crestfallen but with a little bit of that good old northern optimism, we keep walking and walking and just as we are about to surrender to the kebab shop we see it – a full-on nightclub. The line is round the block and the punters look totally different from any others we've seen so far tonight, or in fact anywhere in real life – a nun on roller skates, a group of girls with punk hair, a seven-foot Chinese man in a tank top holding court with a drag queen . . . *Should we attempt it as a last-chance saloon? Nothing to lose at this point.* Little do I realise that my fate is well and truly set and my life is about to change forever.

'Let's try and get in that one,' I say to the others, pointing at the motley crew all chatting and seemingly having a ball in the line on the corner of Princess Street. Andrew, who likes to tie his laces on every street corner it seems, looks up, and reads out the sign of the club: Paradise Factory.

OK. I need to get in this place. I HAVE to get in this place. Not only is this an actual gay nightclub but I hear it's where the cool and crème de le crème of Manchester's nightlife go, from pop stars to actors and even that famous music manager sometimes. I have to get in, I have to get in – please, God, let us in!

'Oh wow,' I say, trying to contain my excitement and not let on that I know it's a hedonistic gay club and that I'm secretly gay myself. 'Sounds fun. Let's do it, guys!' I say, a little too eager. We look at each other nervously, take a few last swigs of our Breakers lager cans that we bought for a bit of Dutch courage and head over to the end of the queue. Andrew, who at this stage in life is very much the shyer one, seems a bit apprehensive, which is fair considering the last two attempts of getting in anywhere have fallen flat as a pancake. But before I can try to convince him it's worth a go, Sean saves the day/night by saying, 'Look, don't worry, leave it to me and Ant to do the talking at the door and just stay behind us, OK?'

As we huddle in close to the now-moving line, the heavy bass and vocals of Robin S's 'Show Me Love' pump out onto the street. *Deep breaths. Let's not fuck this one up* . . . I clock a butch-looking woman holding a torch and the words 'eight pound' being said – must be the entry fee, so I tell the lads to get their cash out just in case she lets us through. The music gets louder, and I'm now face to face with Mother Bouncer who looks me up and down while looking over my shoulder at the other two. 'You do know this is a gay club, lads? You can only come in if you're gay.' *Jesus, does this mean she's overlooked the age thing and we could be in with a chance, then? What about the gay part, though? Do I pretend in front of the other two or tell the truth?!* Now, at this point as far the others in question are concerned, I am, *ahem*, straight. Sean actually *is* straight and Andrew has recently announced over the summer that he is bisexual, 'Like Morrissey and Brett Anderson.' Seeing as I'm at the front and therefore official spokesperson of our sexuality – and the fact that Andrew is at any moment about to spontaneously combust with nerves – I somehow smile at her and say, 'Yes we are,' and with that the three of us get stamped on our wrists and get let through like cattle into the abyss of what can only be described as a fantasy world of the loudest music I've ever heard and enough dry ice to give *Stars in Their Eyes* a run for their money – 'Tonight, Matthew, I will be . . . going to a gay nightclub!'

* * *

My heart beats fast as we make our way through muscled shirtless gay guys to get to the bar, the sound system now pumping through my body. I'd never been around so many gay people in my life, and although I'm nervous there's a sense of freedom and joy and . . . acceptance. Andrew, having now calmed down a bit, also seems mesmerised by it all. 'Oh my God, Anthony, I can't believe we got in. What's that bleach smell, though?' The bleach smell he's referring to I would later come to learn is 'poppers', or amyl nitrate to use the proper description, and boy did all these guys love sniffing them from what I can see and smell. We get our beers and make our way through the sweaty bodies while trying to find a place to base ourselves, and find a big speaker by where we can stand, or more to the point hide, while we make sense of this new glorious underworld we are now right in the middle of. Sean, as always, needs to pee and insists on finding the 'bog'.

'We'll wait here but make sure you come back straight away to this spot,' I shout in his ear over the intro to Deee-Lite's 'Groove Is in the Heart' which has just started up

'Course I will,' he shouts back. 'Just stay there.'

With that he disappears through the smoke while we nod to the music, not quite believing where we actually are. It's too loud for me to talk with Andrew who by now is thankfully a bit more relaxed in our little corner. Scoping out the place and its cast of interesting characters,

5

I spot a little area slightly below us, a few steps down from the dance floor. My eyes are immediately drawn to the man standing there. He appears shirtless, like the majority of the guys inside, and is confidently smoking a cigarette with a crowd of men around him all vying for his attention. He chats casually to a couple of guys either side of him while dancing on the spot. Through the smoke of cigarettes, the dry ice and the constant flashing of the disco lights, it's hard to really see his face. But I suddenly have this overwhelming feeling that this person is him – the powerful and great Oz – aka a hugely successful manager I'd dreamed of meeting one day.

Andrew starts talking to me in my ear about something or other but he may as well be speaking in Cantonese, as I can't concentrate on anything else other than that The Manager was here and I had to talk to him.

'I need a wee now as well. I'll see where our Sean is too. DON'T MOVE,' I say/shout to Andrew.

And like a magnetic force, I begin to make my way across the dance floor, not taking my eyes off the man for a second, in fear that he's some kind of mirage that's about to disappear before I have my chance. Moving into the sea of glistening sweaty torsos I try to think what I'm going to say to him, and then suddenly our eyes meet. In that moment, time stands still. He was looking right at me. *It's him, it's really him.*

In a trance-like state, our eyes lock on to each other. He holds my stare so I let my feet take over my body, walking closer until I'm right opposite him. This is the same man I had told my classmates was my manager and that I was going to be in his new boy band (despite never having met this man before). It was almost as if the more I said it to people the truer it became, to the point that I almost believed it myself; but now, here I am a few metres away from him. It's almost like every single star has aligned to this exact moment, yet I've not a clue what to say to him.

The adrenaline shoots through my body and it feels like everything is in slow motion. 'Hello,' I say. 'I've been trying to find you,' I add cheekily.

'Oh yeah?' he replies, with a genuine smile that suddenly makes me feel calmer, regardless of the fact this is all way too good be true and actually happening.

'Yeah, I signed up for modelling classes at your old agency but then someone told me you've got a different one now,' I ramble, leaning into his ear, our faces touching.

'Yeah, that's right.' He pulls back and looks at me as if he was waiting to say something else.

'I'm Anthony,' I say, realising I hadn't actually introduced myself.

And with that, he leans in and suddenly we're kissing. Not just a little smooch but full-on. A real snog. I had never kissed a man before, and apart from the odd dare behind the bike sheds and an awkward encounter with a second cousin once, I had no experience of kissing girls either.

The kiss feels nothing like kissing a girl. It's harder, but more sensual and natural to me. Once we stop I stand there staring at him in a state of shock.

'You're a bit short to be a model,' he says, almost half joking.

'I'm not a model,' I say, 'I'm a singer. That's why I've been trying to find you. To give you one of my tapes.'

The Manager raises his eyebrows. I'm not sure if he's going to kiss me again or tell me to piss off. He reaches into his jeans pocket and hands me his business card.

I stare at it as though I've found the last golden ticket. I look back up at him, he smiles and says, 'That's the number for my office. Give them a call on Monday and tell them you're dropping a tape off.'

'OK, cool. I'd better get back to my mates. You won't forget me, will you?' I say, trying not to sound too desperate.

He shakes his head, 'Don't worry. I won't, chicken,' (a term of endearment from him I'd get used to in the future).

I turn round, clinging on to the business card for dear life, and head back to Andrew and Sean. 'Where did you go?!' asks Andrew.

'I got lost. It's crazy in here!'

'We need to stick together. Who was that man I saw you talking to?'

My stomach drops. *Fuck. Did he see me kiss him?*

'Oh *him*?!' I say, while trying to figure out what my answer is. Just as well the deafening music is making any real conversation impossible.

'Who is he?' shouts Andrew, looking over the dance floor at the first man I've ever kissed.

'He's a big music manager and this is his business

card.' I hold the card up to their faces. They stare at it, completely blank.

I put the card carefully in my jacket pocket.

'And I'm gonna be a pop star.'

* * *

My new red Casio watch tells me it's 5:01am when I wake the next morning, still a bit drunk and bursting for a pee. Within seconds the flashbacks of the night before arrive. I feel shocked yet elated. I empty my bladder, and creep back to my bedroom and begin rummaging for my jean jacket, praying that this wasn't a dream and that I still have the business card The Manager gave me. I reach into the left pocket but there's just my bus ticket, and nothing in the right pocket. *SHIT*. I scramble for my jeans which are half under the duvet and half on the floor. I say a quick prayer to St Anthony:

'Thank you, St Anthony, for finding the business card.'

I'd been told as an altar boy that I must always pray to St Anthony if I lose something important, but to make sure to thank him in advance to show belief that my prayer will be answered.

I grab the jeans and without even giving them a shake the card falls out along with an empty Hubba Bubba wrapper.

Now that I've found his card it dawns on me that there is in fact no demo tape of me singing in existence and I have to somehow come up with one. Talk about 'fake it till you make it'!

I know that Forsyth's, the music shop in town, sells backing tracks to sing along to (mostly for karaoke). However, I've spent all my final McDonald's wages before being fired on *Smash Hits* magazines, new trainers and the latest Kylie Minogue CD. Even if I had the money, I've got no idea where you would even get recording equipment, let alone how to use it, so I need to get creative with what I already have. Basically, my future now depends on a cheap microphone and my hi-fi.

My sister Angela bought me one of her favourite albums from the car boot recently: *Songs in the Key of Life* by Stevie Wonder. I love Stevie Wonder, and this album is special and I haven't stopped playing it all week. The first track on the album is a mid-tempo song called 'Love's In Need', and I've had it on repeat.

I've only got one shot at impressing The Manager and need to showcase my voice as best as I can. It would have been easier to go with a generic pop song but there's something about this track that makes me feel something, and the tone somehow suits my voice. It also starts *a cappella* (without music), which is both a risk and a bonus. Still slightly hungover but determined, I do the best I can and make the demo. I'm useless at anything technical – ask me to play you a song on the piano and I can mysteriously just do it by ear, but not this type of stuff, so I end up being surprised that I pull it off. I layer the backing vocals line by line, recording tape-to-tape on the hi-fi. I then copy the harmonies that are on the original record and pray to God that The Manager will like it. It takes all day but I go to bed with a sense of achievement – at least now I've actually made a physical tape as opposed to just trying to will one into existence. Now all I need to do is call the office tomorrow and ask when I can drop it off. Needless to say, I don't sleep a wink that night.

With my job at McDonald's now being in the bin (along with the stolen fish sandwich), I spend the morning plucking up the courage to make the call. Mum, God bless her, hasn't paid the phone bill again this month, which means we are only allowed incoming calls. Luckily there's a phone box on my estate. Around lunchtime, with business card in hand, I rummage through the fruit bowl (the one that only has a plastic banana in it) for a handful of change and run to the phone box. I dial the number of the agency and wait.

'Hi there, my name is Anthony . . . Can I speak to The Manager, please?' I say, trying my best to sound as mature and professional as I can in a piss-stinking phone box with no door.

'He's in a meeting at the moment, what is it regarding?'

'Erm . . .' The woman on the other end's response throws me. 'He told me to call him today about a demo tape, I—'

'Sorry, love, we only accept demo tapes by post. I can give you the address.' I can almost hear her sympathetic smile over the phone and her tone of voice telling me she probably has hundreds of calls like this one every week.

'But I saw him at the weekend and he told me to call him.' I've come this far . . .

She hesitated.

'Please hold,' she says through imagined gritted teeth.

The beep of the 'on hold' sound seems to go on forever, and I fear the worst. I wonder if he's forgotten about me. Have I got it wrong? Maybe he gave his card to everyone just to shut them up. A group of lads from the estate start playing football on the grass near the phone box. I keep my eye on them in fear of being called a 'poof' as usual.

'Hi there, sorry to keep you waiting. Just connecting you now.'

I take a deep breath and wait.

'Hello?'

His voice sounds different than it did in the club. But then again, our only exchange had been shouting in each other's ears over loud music. He sounds hoarse, but friendly.

'Hi,' I say confidently, as though we're life-long friends. 'It's Anthony, we met on Saturday at Paradise Factory. You gave me your card. I'm the singer.'

'Hello, chicken, how are you?'

Phew. He *does* remember me.

'I'm good, thanks. Was just wondering when was a good time to drop my demo tape off?' Using the words 'demo tape' makes me feel like the real deal, even if I had just used whatever I could cobble together and recorded it in my bedroom.

'You can drop it off tomorrow if you want. I won't be here because I'm at *Top of the Pops*, but I'll let Pam on reception know you're coming.'

Suddenly it all felt real. *Top of the Pops*? Pam from reception? *Oh. My. God.*

'OK, that's great. I'll bring it in tomorrow,' I say, trying to keep my cool and not squeal with excitement.

'Make sure you leave your phone number,' he finishes, in his warm raspy tone. *Thank God for incoming calls.* Although I would have waited all day in the phone box for him to call if I had to.

'Will do.'

'Ta-ra,' he says, sounding more like Vera Duckworth than some big music manager.

'OK, bye.' I hang the phone back on the receiver and try to contain my excitement for the future and the possibility that this could really be my chance to make it.

I'm soon brought back down to earth when I return home for tea. Mother has somehow managed to burn my curry Pot Noodle while attempting to 'keep it warm' in the microwave. I can't remember much about the rest of that week apart from the fact one of the receptionists *did* call and I was indoors to receive it this time. An appointment is set up for the Friday to meet The Manager. He wants to meet me. *Holy shit.*

Having no actual job to go to I spend the week convinced he's going to change his mind and call to cancel. I almost wish I was still at McDonald's, even though I hated it, at least it would have taken my mind off all this worrying. I still can't believe I got fired. The day it happened the area manager Yvette was on with me and she was a miserable cow at the best of times.

We had already had an altercation over the ratio of how the fries were to be stacked in the fryer, and no matter how quick I tried I just couldn't get the timing right for the infamous 'cheesecall' (any past or current Maccy D employees, I feel your pain). The issue with the 'cheesecall' was that if you hadn't cooked the burger in time for the cheese to go on, then it would be classed as a waste of a burger and have to go straight into the bin . . . but not just any bin, a 'clean' bin only for lukewarm food that was still in its wrapper. I thought this was a cardinal sin. Why couldn't it be given to the homeless, or at least let us eat it? After a disastrous try-out on the till during rush hour – I think Yvette put me there on purpose after me telling her the lame excuse I wasn't great with 'numbers and people' – I was a nervous wreck, so snuck into the back when the thought of sneaking a Filet-O-Fish crossed my mind. The dreaded lunchtime rush of customers had subsided so I decided to throw caution to the wind and delve into the bin when no one was looking. Halfway through the sandwich I heard a voice scream:

'Under NO circumstances must a worker eat the contents of the clean food bin.'

'Oh, I was just . . .' I squirmed, tartare sauce dripping down my chin.

'I repeat, NO circumstances, Anthony. You are dismissed with immediate effect.'

I suddenly felt a strange sense of relief. I didn't know it then but I did have bigger fish to fry after all, which seemed quite fitting as I gulped the last bite.

NICE TO MEET ME

There are no two ways about it, Arnold isn't getting any better and I feel helpless. The closest feeling I've had to this is when Nana was sick and we found out she had cancer, and just like then, my dad is trying to reassure me, even though we both know it's not looking good.

'All cats get sick from time to time, son,' he says, while ironing the collar on my Pepe Jeans denim jacket that he's washed by hand in the sink and dried on the radiator overnight so I can wear it to my big meeting with The Manager today.

'I know, Dad, it's just that he's not eaten in days now and he looks so weak and . . .'

'Now listen, Anthony,' he interrupts, which is rare for my dad, the most patient man in the world.

'Today is your big day, you have got to focus on that. I'll boil some chicken for him later. He likes that. He gobbled up the whole lot last time. It might be that

15

cheap cat food your mother's been getting that's not agreeing with him.'

I'm not buying it. Arnold has never been sick like this, but I can see Dad's worried I'm distressed, so I play along with his optimism.

'OK, let's see how it goes with the chicken, it's probably just a bug.'

I'm not sure who's comforting who, but he is right. I cannot blow this opportunity. I must stay strong. I contemplate which shirt I'll wear out of the three Dad's already ironed and laid out on the bed. The choices are the plain black one I bought from this new cool American store called Gap, the white Fruit of the Loom one, or the navy blue one that fits best which my mum bought me from Asda's 'George' range. I settle on the Gap one; plus, everyone looks good in black. It's also *very* slimming. Just as well I stuck to my new diet and fitness plan over the summer. Who knew that restricting myself to a thousand calories a day and using my bedside cabinet as a Stairmaster for 30 minutes while watching *Brookside* would get rid of all that weight? The Mandy Jordache 'husband under the patio' storyline hasn't done any harm either to keeping me exercising – perseverance does pay off after all. The suntan from my summer in St Ives staying with my sister Angela and brother-in-law Clint along with the new buzzcut Clint gave me haven't done any harm either.

The 163 bus to Manchester Piccadilly arrives just in time. I pay my 50-pence bus fare and head up to the back seat on the top. I like getting the bus at this time as it's never that busy and even if it is, there's never any trouble. I take out The Manager's business card to check the address – even though I could walk there backwards with my eyes closed by now – and to confirm that I am not in some kind of waking dream that I will soon come to my senses from.

A gazillion thoughts run through my head. *What is he going to say to me? Is he going to ask me to audition for his next boy band? Will we kiss again? I hope so.*

I whisper a prayer so the nosy woman from Howarth's cake shop – the one near us that my mum put a claim in for slipping on an overflowing mop bucket and won – who just got on the bus doesn't hear me:

'Thank you, St Anthony, for finding me the . . . er . . . the . . . confidence to make The Manager . . . want me. Amen.'

Not sure that quite cuts it in the sincerest of prayer requests department, but St Ant knows my intentions are good. He also helped me find the business card in the first place after I thought I'd lost it, so he must be on my side.

I get off the bus on Oldham Street just outside the Vinyl Exchange, which is one of my fave places to go for second-hand CDs and old records, and head towards Piccadilly Gardens, which still gives me anxiety from when I was mugged there aged 12 by two rough lads who asked me for the time, and when I went to look at my watch – a new Swatch watch I'd only just got for my birthday – shoved their hands in my shell suit jacket and took my £5 – that I'd also only just got for my birthday

– and ran off. It's the quickest way to cut through the city centre, though, so I keep my head down and walk fast. The chances of being robbed twice in the same spot must be slim, especially today of *all* days.

I nip into Boots on Cross Street to have a quick spritz of aftershave they've got on display. When I was in close contact with The Manager in the nightclub on Saturday he smelled amazing, so I want to up my aftershave game. I could smell it on my T-shirt the next day along with the cigarette smoke and them bloody poppers that were wafting in the air. God knows what he thought of my scent. I doubt my Lynx Java made a lasting impression. I notice a bottle that's being promoted in a mysterious dark blue bottle with a sun-kissed Adonis rising from the sea on the poster: 'Davidoff – Cool Water.' I spray it on both sides on my neck and on my wrist. It smells a bit strong, but it'll do.

I arrive at the office early, so stand in the ginnel a few hundred yards down from the entrance to kill some time. I don't want to look too eager. City centre office workers rush by going to get their lunches, and a homeless man selling *The Big Issue* clocks me. I wonder if I'm in his spot. Maybe the still-half-full two-litre bottle of Diamond White cider that's staring at me on the floor is his and he thinks I'm going to pinch it. He doesn't need to worry about that. Apart from the fact it's probably got his spit in it and tastes like battery acid, why would I want that at this time of day? *I could do with a bit of Dutch courage, but Jesus.*

I check myself over one last time: trainer laces

tucked in behind socks, jeans pulled over tongue of trainers again, and only two middle buttons fastened on the denim jacket (just like Keanu Reeves had his on the cover of *SKY* magazine) and I'm ready as I'll ever be. After years of dreaming about being a pop star and telling everyone I would be one, I was going for an official meeting with The Manager of one of the biggest pop bands in the UK. I'm still not exactly sure what this meeting's all about, but whatever it is I know it's a chance of a lifetime. For some reason I'm not as nervous going into the office as I was when I phoned. I press the buzzer on the intercom.

'Hi, can I help?'

'Oh, hello, it's Anthony for . . .'

'Come on up, love.'

Love. She called me 'love'.

I walk up the two flights of stairs and enter the main reception. I notice a wobbly MTV award, and lovely Pam greets me with a smile. She looks like she's been to the Bahamas for a week.

'Hi, Pam, you look well.'

It's totally fine for me to use first-name terms, since she just called me 'love'.

'Costa del tanning shop on Deansgate, love.'

Love again, *and* now cracking jokes. I'm well in.

'Take a seat. He'll be with you shortly. Can I get you a tea or coffee?'

Blimey. This is going better than I thought.

'Tea, please, milk no sugar.'

Pam trots off to the kitchen, her silver slingbacks

clicking as she goes, and I sit on one of the Chesterfield leather sofas in reception. I knows it's a Chesterfield sofa because my mum always has to show me the same one she can't afford in the Freemans catalogue she looks through nightly, while I pray to God she doesn't notice that a page of the men's underwear section has been ripped out.

'Here you go, love. Tea, milk no sugar.'

I'm now starting to wonder if Pam has forgotten my name and is just replacing it with 'love' instead. I should have known; she's probably seen hundreds of 'me's' coming in to see The Manager, all hoping for a golden ticket to fame. It's just a normal day to her.

I pick up a magazine called *Music Week* and I suddenly feel very professional. It's got the charts at the back – not just one chart but loads of different ones. I flick through to what looks like the main pop chart. How is anyone still buying Wet Wet Wet's 'Love Is All Around'? It's even got the number of weeks it's been number one: 17?! One week in the top 10 would do me. I wonder if this band I might be auditioning for have to write their own songs? What if we have to dance? I hope it's a cool band. Maybe it's a duo? We could be the new China Black! Then again, maybe not.

I hear a man's voice and footsteps coming towards the reception area. He's shouting back to someone in the office, probably his PA, about someone else: 'He forgets where he's from,' and, 'He's too busy buying bloody antiques with Elton.' I think it's The Manager and he sounds pissed off about someone. I pretend to be reading intently on the page I've now landed on, which happens to be a profile of the singer in new band Let Loose discussing their recent chart success. I keep my eyes focused on the page to appear natural, although I'm baffled by one of their names.

'Lead singer, Richie Wermerling.'

All anxiousness over The Manager approaching subsides for a second while my brain tries to compute where such a name comes from. It's not your usual name for a pop star. It sounds more like a character Roald Dahl would be proud of: 'Little Richie Wermerling was a strange and curious child, who, unlike the other children in class who brought their packed lunches to school every day, would rush home to eat his daily cabbage and snail pie with crow's beak tart for afters . . .'

'Hello, chicken.'

I snap out of my bizarre Roald Dahl/Let Loose daydream to see The Manager welcoming me with a possibly flirty but definitely happy-to-see-me expression on his face.

'Oh. Hi,' I reply enthusiastically.

'Come on through to my office.'

With that I follow him through what seems to be a mini kitchen area. 'This is Ying,' says The Manager, gesturing to a cool-looking Chinese girl in jeans and a white T-shirt. I assume she's a model and wonder what she's doing rinsing a cup in the sink. 'She looks after my artists,' he says, making sure I know who's the boss round here. I wonder if she knows something I don't. Maybe he's told her about me and my demo tape. Maybe she's one of those PAs? Imagine having your very own PA?! Would I get someone looking after me like that?

The Manager walks in front of me. I can't help looking at his cool grey low-waist jeans with the silver Armani logo on the back. He smells the same too, the same aftershave from when we met. Gold and platinum discs adorn the walls and another huge Chesterfield stretches out opposite a window with a mini balcony, the balcony I've looked up at a dozen times wondering what it would take to actually be on the other side of it. I'm that awestruck I don't notice there's someone else sat in his office at her own desk facing the window.

'Izzy, I'm about to have a meeting so make sure no one bothers me.'

Izzy, the woman with her own desk in his office, and who now appears to be seven foot five when standing, gathers her papers like her life depends on it and leaves the room.

'Close the door.'

The door slams a little too loud for my nervous system, but judging by Izzy's demeanour that's just how she shuts doors.

'Right, then.'

OK, here we go. He's about to tell me the demo tape was a load of crap, or he's found out I'm only 16 and is going to tell the police I shouldn't have been in a nightclub.

'Is that really you on that tape?'

'Yeah, it's me. I spent all weekend making it. I know

the quality's not great, but I recorded it all on my hi-fi with a . . .'

'It's brilliant. Who else is singing on it, though?'

The Manager doesn't seem to understand that it's all me on the tape, that the backing vocals are all my voice and that I used two cassettes to bounce down each harmony part with my sister's karaoke machine microphone.

'It's me on all of it. I did it *a cappella*.'

I hope he follows what I mean by throwing in this intellectual musical term, one I learned from the album notes of Soul II Soul's *Club Classics Vol. One*. I wait for his response.

'Well, I'm very impressed, Anthony. You've got a brilliant voice. Very soulful.'

Phew.

'Thing is, I'm not looking for another pop band.'

Oh shit.

'I think you've got what it takes to be a solo artist, how do you feel about that?'

Is he joking? How do I feel?

'Well, yeah. I feel great about that. I mean, er, yes!'

With that, he slides some (already prepared) papers from under what looks like a mini crystal ball paperweight and hands them to me across the desk.

I contemplate cracking a joke about the crystal ball-looking thing, and that my mother reads tea leaves for five pound a cup, and that she can do his if he wants, but I keep schtum and pretend I know what the words 'development deal' mean.

He goes on to explain that within this three-page document is a basic agreement between him and me and that for the next six months I will 'work' in the management office and get to see how everything runs while also starting work with music producers and writing my own songs at home every night. If it all goes well, we will then go to record labels and I will get a record deal and be a solo artist.

'You can write songs, can't you? You said you play piano, right?'

As this question could clearly be a make-or-break situation, I lie and say:

'Oh yes, I write all the time. I *love* writing songs, I just don't have any real equipment to record on, you see.'

'OK, well, we can sort that out.'

To be honest I'm not *actually* lying – I once wrote a song with my best friend John at primary school called 'Slave to Fashion'. We performed it as a duo in a Halloween-themed talent competition, which my mother conveniently sabotaged by making some kind of illicit agreement with Mrs Spooner the head teacher to show off her singing talents in return for a private tea-cup reading, culminating in her 'surprising' the other parents in the audience by bursting into 'As Long As He Needs Me' from *Oliver!* right before the results were called. Mortified.

'I'll need to come to yours and meet your mum and dad before you sign anything. It's important they know and feel comfortable that you're in safe hands.'

I can't imagine this man's silver BMW parked on our council estate, nor can I imagine what state the house is going to be in. There's no way it can happen today.

'I was also thinking . . .'

Go on, I'm all ears. I already feel like I've won the jackpot. I can double up as office cleaner if you need me to.

'Your name – Anthony Kavanagh – it's a bit long-winded for a pop star. I think you should just have one name. All the big solo artists have just one name, like Prince, Madonna, Elvis . . .'

I'm liking the sound of this but I don't think 'Anthony' will be selling out Wembley Arena any time soon.

'What about "Kavanagh" without the "GH" so it's "Kavana"? Sounds a bit like Keanu, as in Keanu Reeves – you look a bit like him.'

The denim jacket worked, then.

'OK, then – sure!'

I'm not exactly going to disagree with anything The Manager says at this point, as long as I get my foot in the door.

'Why don't you sit at my desk and call your mum and dad and tell them I'm going to drive you home and come to meet them for a cup of tea and a chat. I'll leave you in here while I pop upstairs.'

I walk to the other side of the desk and take a seat. The chair swivels round and is made of black leather. I feel powerful. I feel invincible. Like JR Ewing from *Dallas*, soon to be taking over my very own pop empire of the charts!

I call home and Mum answers. She just got in from afternoon bingo and she's about to find out her son is going to be a pop star.

'Hi, Mum. I met The Manager today and he wants to sign me, and he wants to meet you and Dad tonight when he drives me home from the office where I am now.'

Silence.

'Mum, you there?'

'Sorry, love, your father's boil-in-the-bag fish in butter sauce is bubblin' over the pissin' pan.'

She's no Delia Smith.

'Yes, love. Manager. Yes. Fine. I'll spray some air freshener round and put the heating on. Ta-ra.'

The Manager pops his head round to see if I'm finished.

'Everything OK with your mum and dad?'

I tell him they are looking forward to meeting him in a bit and pray she at least gives the carpet a once-over with the hoover.

'I want you to come and say hello to my staff.'

I follow The Manager up the winding staircase to the next level. It's a lot noisier with phones ringing and photocopiers bleeping. He waits at the top of the stairs while I catch up, too busy reading what's engraved on the gold and platinum discs on the walls. I reach the top and he gently puts his hand on my waist to guide me in. I feel nervous yet safe. Not sure I've felt so happy or whatever this feeling is in a long time, or if ever.

'Everyone, I want you to meet my new artist, Kavana. He's going to be working in the office for a few months with you all. We will call him "Kav" for short.'

A mini sea of faces smile and shout 'Hi, Kav!' in unison and I wave and say 'Hi' back, attempting to make eye contact with each one while my head moves round like a nodding dog at each soon-to-be-familiar face. Little do they know I have just become an imposter in my own body, answering to a name that's not really mine, yet every part of me is ready to take it on and forget who I really am. Me erased.

'Well, it's nice to meet you all!' I say, feeling half fraud and half sincere lottery winner.

'I suppose we'd better get you home, then. I've never been to Moston.' The Manager laughs, as we take the other stairs back down and get ready to leave.

'Is there a toilet I can use?'

He points me to it and I go inside and shut the door. I don't really need the toilet, I just need a moment to myself to take in what's just happened.

I turn on the cold-water tap so it sounds like I'm making use of the facilities and catch a glimpse of my own reflection in the mirror above the sink. I imagine what I must have looked like saying my new name to the office staff. I mouth the words a few times to see.

Hi, I'm Kav.

Hi . . . I'm Kav.

HI.

I'M.

KAV.

A new identity is mine.

It's nice to meet me.

COUNCIL HOUSE
MEMORIES

'm not sure what cloud on cuckoo land I was floating on when coming up with this whole pop-star fantasy, but I seem to have forgotten about the minor detail of 'me being gay and how I deal with it'. It's one thing hiding your true inner workings to friends and family, but putting myself out there for all the world to see is another. I've kept up the act of being straight since I knew I was gay aged 10 years old when I started getting feelings for a boy in my class at school. I would go home and think of being with him – not like that, I just wanted to be close to him and I'd get butterflies whenever I'd see him in class, something I'd never felt with my other friends who were mainly all girls. Now I'm all grown up maybe I thought that officially becoming a pop star in the making would suddenly mean I'd become immune to any sexual feeling towards males, as though having my big dream come true would be enough to satisfy every part of me. Spoiler alert: it hasn't. In fact, ever since I met The Manager these feelings have reached a whole new intensity. Instead, there's this longing inside of me that's all-consuming. When he's distant, or doesn't give me attention, I'm a melancholy mess. The lines between professionalism and desire were blurred from the beginning, and I feel stuck. We should never have kissed that first time, but let's be real, I didn't exactly push him away. I think all of it came to a head around the time we had our last catch-up meeting. These were not like the after-hours ones we had in his office when all his staff had left. I'm talking about the official ones that are booked in his diary and that I don't really look forward to . . .

This one started with his PA Izzy – 'with a Z, remember!' – announcing over the intercom that it's time for our chat. I hover awkwardly in the kitchen area, pretending to look busy, while he stays in his office, making me wait. Eventually we head to the Pizza Express on the corner, making small talk while I secretly panic about having to eat in front of him. I order the margarita for cutting ease while he always goes for the Fiorentina without olives. He talks business, while pointing out which of the new demos he likes, and I nod eagerly, desperate for validation. 'Key change at the end, definitely,' and, 'Shorter middle eight, I agree' (I don't). He orders a Diet Coke and lights a menthol Consulate, while I order a sparkling water to appear sophisticated. He offers me one of his menthols, which

I accept, regretting it instantly as the nicotine spikes my anxiety and ruins the tiny bit of appetite I already don't have. He flirts with the same muscly waiter from the gay village he knows, and I feel sick with jealousy on top of the cigarette. We skip dessert and he pays. But this time was different – this time he told he loved me. 'I love you now,' to be precise. 'Now' since he's gotten to know me, believe in me, and care for me, he said. No one's ever told me they love me before – not even Mum and Dad, though I know they do. But him loving me? That changes a lot. Surely it means there's a chance we could be together. I want to tell him I love him too, in fact I think I'm in love with him. I must not have these feelings though. I must not allow it. He is 20 years older, has the sweetest partner, and I just can not and will not be gay. It's all in my head. It can't happen and it won't happen. We walk back to the office in what feels like an awkward silence. No doubt it will be back to being professional once we get inside. I go to the kitchen and put the kettle on for the coffees no ones asked for and he saunters back to his big office and shuts the door, the scent of his aftershave lingering in the air. I wish this pop star stuff would hurry up.

11 Months Later – October, 1995

The word 'love' hasn't been mentioned again, and this literal straitjacket I seem to have found myself wearing feels suffocating. It's odd, as no one in the office asks me if I've got a girlfriend, or who I fancy. I naively think that it's probably out of respect, as they know fame is on the horizon and that they will probably end up working for me soon. As long as they don't think I'm not being genuine. I'd hate that. Since working in the office as tea boy I've become an expert at steering the conversation away from anything remotely personal, but it's bloody exhausting. I suppose I'd better get used to it. So far, it's still only The Manager who is in on the secret but he seems to have stopped wanting to show me affection lately. The 6pm chats when everyone goes home have come to an end and I don't understand why. My emotions are heavy, and I don't like seeing him with other potential clients from the agency. Especially the ones that look like male models. *How can I compete with that? I know he's attracted to me and genuinely believes in my talent, but my arms are skinny, and I don't have the athletic frame of these other guys.*

The last six months have been a mix of excitement and anticipation, but it's also been a time of having to be patient. *Ugh.* I do like being in the hustle and bustle of the office every day, but other than making cups of tea and coffee and going on the lunch run there's not much else for me to do. I sometimes wonder if The Manager's promise of making me a star will ever come to fruition, but surely it has to? At least I've been pouring myself into the songwriting. Another item that's been put on the tab until one of these big deals he's negotiating comes through has been my new Fostex 4-Track Portastudio. I never in a million years would have thought I'd have the technical abilities to work something like that, but so far so good. I've not been entirely sure what to write about, being someone who's never been in a proper relationship – who am I kidding, *any* relationship of the romantic kind – so I've mainly been imagining what love is like and doing it that way. That is until last night. I wrote a song about The Manager. It just came out of nowhere. I can't tell him but I hope he somehow realises it. I also hope calling it 'Release It' doesn't appear too rude, as I'm describing feelings – mainly his about me to be made clearer. One minute he tells me he loves me then he goes cold, almost ignoring me. He needs to be careful what he's wished for. I may have found a secret power in this songwriting malarkey. Don't they say you're supposed to write about what you know anyway?

Release it
Go with the flow
Release it
I know what you know
You talk like tomorrow is light years away
You're constantly playing safe
When you get affection, you have it your way
While I just sit and wait
We break every rule
So why do you choose to be serious?
Let it out
Can you release it?

I made the demo at home and we sat and played it in his office the next day. Sally stayed for the listening session too, but gave no indication of what she thought until she got the green light from the expression on the face of the man who pays her wages. When The Manager said, 'Love the R&B vibe,' Izzy went along by saying, 'Totally,' and nodding out of time with her eyes closed like she was meditating. I tend to stare at the floor at times like this – where are you supposed to look when listening to your own songs? Especially when it's about the person sat directly in front of you who seems oblivious to it. Needless to say, there wasn't one comment about the lyrics, but I was told: 'This has to go on the album.'

The confusion and longing continued, but I'm on a roll. I go home and write another one, and another, like a glutton for punishment, this time in an attempt to make it more obvious I'm in love, or at least think I'm in love with him, with titles such as 'Holdin' Back On U' (very Prince of me), 'The Time Is Right' and 'Where Are You?' – all songs that will eventually make the album cut. At this juncture my career isn't even my focus anymore – I'm too consumed with wanting to be with him. I'm moody and unpredictable at home, snapping at Mum and Dad. They know I write songs when I'm locked in my room but have no clue they're about the man they've trusted with my future, and indirectly, theirs too.

* * *

It's decided that a soon-to-be pop star shouldn't be living in a council house. Since I'm not really old enough to have my own place yet, The Manager's offered to loan me the money to buy a little place for me and the folks. It will once again go on the 'tab' – a huge gesture, proof that he's not messing around. No one lends you £50k unless they're sure it's getting paid back. Sally, the more maternal PA, got on the case to help us find somewhere. When I broke the news to Mum and Dad that their son is buying them a house, they didn't exactly jump for joy. I was met with, 'We can't move at our age,' and, 'We love it round here.' I understand that they're of a certain age (that's what you get for having a child in your forties) and change isn't easy for them, but they need to understand that I already feel threatened by some of the lads round ours when walking to the bus stop, so imagine how bad it will be when I'm on TV? I sometimes wonder if they have any clue of what's really coming. One thing that definitely *was* coming was my 18th birthday, and I was going to have the party of all parties. Family, old school pals and all the new crew. I told myself, *This time next year it's going to be a very different story, so I want my last birthday before everyone knows my name to go out with a bang, to be one I'll always remember.*

WAITING

Months pass and I am still yet to sign the record deal. The Manager tells me it has nothing to do with me or the labels not being interested, it's more that he's waiting for the exact right deal to be negotiated. The good news is my publishing deal with EMI as a songwriter is being finalised as we speak, which will give me a £150,000 advance which they will then recoup back from my future worldwide songwriting royalties. It's a lot to make sense of, especially considering it wasn't that long ago I was flipping beef patties and the only thing I had trouble working out was the ratio of cheese slices to gherkins on a Big Mac.

I must try and be patient. I'm so thankful The Manager is doing all this for me.

I mean, I must remember the hundreds of demos that land in the office every month and he chose *me*. Mum says I must trust what The Manager is doing and he will get me the right record deal when the time is right.

The development deal I signed with him was only for six months, though, and that's run out, so there is no official contract in place between us anymore – except for the unspoken one, of course. *No, that's stupid of me. I need to put that stuff to one side. I wish he would give me more, though. Does he want me like that or not?* Just a glance or smile can change my whole week, never mind day. I get so confused. One minute he will flirt with me in front of the office staff but not enough to raise suspicion, and the next he will say something like, 'Look at those child-bearing hips,' like he did in front of Gina, one of the agency staff who was in the kitchen on her lunch break while I was doing the washing up. He was joking but it made me self-conscious. The 'love handles' I've had all my life seem to be the last thing to be going, even after all this new gym work, so it felt mean. Gina saw I was embarrassed and just said 'Aaaw' while clicking her two Canderel sweeteners in the coffee I'd just made her. She's always dieting so she probably didn't like it either. *Maybe I can get liposuction on them. I saw Mick Hucknall had it done but I also read that it makes your whole penis and balls area purple and sore for months. Not that anyone will see them at this rate. I'll just have to work harder at the gym and reduce calories even though I've already reduced to a thousand a day. I could try the bulimia thing, but I hate being sick. I know, I could ask big Denise the stylist who now cuts my hair at Vidal Sassoon where she got those slimming pills she told me about. She lost two stone in a month. She said it made her smoke 60 cigs a day and it felt like she was a having a nervous breakdown, but still, at least she was thin.*

* * *

I hear The Manager on the phone in his office discussing me to more music-exec types, and my mood lifts when I hear him playing my new demos full blast. Such a strange feeling to have one foot in the becoming-a-pop-star world yet still turning up to the office every day as a tea boy.

'Once all this starts your feet won't touch the ground,' he keeps reminding me.

Due to the fact I'm about to turn 18 I start chancing my luck by going to Paradise Factory on the odd weekend in the hope he's there so I can 'bump' into him away from the office. I drag Andrew or whichever friend will tag along with me. The Saturdays I do go he is there with the same guys he was with the first time we collided. All vying for his attention. The difference this time, though, is I'm with him now – I'm his new boy, his artist, his new protégé. Those other lads flocking around him don't have what I have. He is warm and relaxed with me and I feel safe and desired again. It's on one of these Saturday nights I take my first Ecstasy tablet. I'd never touched drugs before then, but I notice The Manager and his close pals (and most of the club) are definitely 'on' something judging by their eyes and blissed-out faces, so I ask if I can have one. I'm told to just take half to begin and wait. Nothing happens, though, at least not for the first 20 minutes, and then, out of nowhere I feel something. A warm sensation in my belly followed by an immediate need to talk and dance and chew gum and connect. WOW. A cigarette tastes amazing too, I want to smoke three in a row. It also makes the alcohol go down a lot easier. I want to keep drinking more and more, not like the others who seem to be happy with bottled water. The stuff gives me a thirst for everything, and I feel invincible. I pop the other half. *Fucking hell, I want this to last forever!*

I'd really only heard about Es when I saw Brian Harvey from East 17 get absolutely crucified for saying he took them, culminating in him being fired from the group. Judging by the stories I've heard about their manager, I think it was unfair. At least my manager is kind and loves me. Even if he doesn't show it sometimes. I feel sorry for Brian, even though it was a stupid thing to say. I hope the press don't twist my words or make fun of me when I get famous.

I soon get the weekend routine down to a fine art, and the pills every Saturday night are the highlight of my week. 'Bumping' into The Manager is a bonus, as when I do see him we will often find a spot away from the others, usually on the third floor where we can have private time. It feels amazing and any fears of not being wanted or desired by him melt in an instant. In that moment I am lost in a sea of, well, ecstasy – it does exactly what it says it on the tin. During the week it's back to business as usual – we don't even mention seeing each other at the club – so I make the most of the weekend attention. I also notice that by Tuesday my mood sinks to an awful, dark low. I overhear Peter from the agency, who is usually out clubbing every weekend, shirtless, up and down Canal Street, say something about 'Suicide Tuesday' like it's a normal thing to go through after taking E on the weekend.

'I'll be ready to party again come Friday, love!' he said.

Judging by my routine of late, I am too.

* * *

Around this time of my semi-hedonistic life at the weekends and office pop-boy-in-waiting during the week, I am sent for singing lessons with a vocal coach called Rhonda. Not because I can't sing, but because, apparently, I must learn how to use my 'instrument' (as she calls it properly) and it will help me when I'm on tour. Rhonda looks like Stevie Nicks and lives in Chorlton in south Manchester in a bohemian-style cluttered flat with various cats. We sing scales up and down the piano and she stands behind me placing her hand on my stomach while I fill my diaphragm, which pops my belly out and makes it look fatter than I already think it is. She tells me she has taught Annie Lennox and gives me some special exercises to warm up the vocal chords. My favourite one being in Italian – '*Barrrrrromaaaaa*,' and repeat '*Barrrooooma*.' I enjoy the dramatics of it and copy the way she rolls her Rs in full effect.

'It's opera!' she tells me while lighting a spliff. 'For

my sciatica!' she adds, whatever that is, while taking three little tokes which she then holds while pinching her nose. 'Bravo for today, sounding wonder-ful!' She sounds like she's inhaled helium rather than Chorlton's finest Ganja, then randomly blows the smoke into the cat-litter tray behind the piano.

'Old trick I learned, neutralises the weed smell! Same time next week?'

I enjoy our weekly Thursday afternoon sessions at 1pm with my new friend Rhonda, and although there is still no record deal in place it gives me hope that this is yet more confirmation I am being prepped for the big time. Or at least something.

THAT LONDON

Autumn, 1995

I've only ever been on a plane once, and that was to Canada. Aunty Anne, on my mum's side, sent me a ticket in the post when I was 11 and I went there all by myself for the six-week summer holidays from school. I spilled the in-flight meal of curry and rice (yes, curry and rice on a plane) all over myself and one of the kind in-flight chaperones had to wipe me down with a wet wipe. I'm not sure whether it was the embarrassment of said food disaster or just madness, but I also decided upon landing that it was a great idea to speak in a Canadian accent for the whole of the six weeks I was there, not letting up once. Still to this day I'm baffled at how not one member of my overseas family asked me why I was talking in such a manner. Maybe they thought I was bit demented. I think I was just wanting to fit in, even if it was a ridiculously over-the-top way to go about it. Even then I wanted to be someone else, it seems.

There are no fake accents today, though. Today I am travelling with The Manager to London or 'That London' as Dad likes to call it, which I believe is a northern term of endearment for the place, even though he's Irish. The Manager spends most of the short flight reading the paper while I munch on the complimentary breakfast of cornflakes with ice-cold milk, nervously balancing them on the pull-down tray in order not to have a repeat of the Canada curry episode. A posh car is sent for us when we land, and we both get in the back and sit in silence. I'm scared to make conversation and feel out of my depth being with The Manager outside of the office environment or intoxicated in a nightclub. He is in a mood, I can tell. I'm glad I have my new Nokia mobile phone to play with, which can also send 'texts' – it's amazing. I decide to text Andrew.

'Greetings from LONDON! YES LONDON!'
'OMG. What you doing there?!'
'With Manager meeting record labels today, eek'
'Oooh Exciting. How is he?'
'Moody. Not sure if it's me, or if he's on comedown from wknd'
'Ha . . . Prob wknd. You worry too much'

Our first stop is to RCA Records to meet an 'A&R' (which I've learned stands for 'artist and repertoire') man called Nick Raymonde – the same man who signed Take That, among other big names. I sit there amazed that I'm actually in a record label office while

The Manager explains I write my own songs and have a voice like Stevie Wonder. *Gulp.*

'He's not just a brilliant songwriter,' says The Manager.

'I can see the girls are going to love him too,' Nick chips in.

I'm not used to this. Where do you look when two powerful music industry execs are talking about you in the most flattering way? The floor, that's where. Or at least I do, until I realise I look like I'm getting a scolding in the head teacher's office or somehow being told off, so I look up again to see both men staring at me, clearly wondering what on earth I'm doing. Nick, probably in sympathy and aware that it may all be a bit daunting, tells me to go for a wander round the big office and the stock cupboards and to 'help yourself to any music'. So I do exactly that, feeling relief that I've been let out of the 'let's make him a pop star' class early. It is a lot, but this is what I've dreamed of, so I better get used to it. I'm being given a chance in a million.

Is this actually happening?!

I wonder what the boy bands do when they meet these bigwigs? They have each other to bounce off, but I've only got me. I'm not complaining, it's just that I hope I'm selling myself right. I suppose in a boy band you've got the serious one, the cute one, the cheeky one, the tough one. Am I supposed to be a mix of all of them?

I open one of the CD cupboards and it feels like Christmas. So many CDs. Hundreds to choose from. New Kylie, M People, Michelle Gayle. I realise my choices are verging on a bit camp, so I throw in a few rock bands to mix it up. Must keep to the straight image. Must remember to keep my voice more 'laddy'-sounding too. Not too rough, but I mustn't sound camp. I'm not camp anyway. I'm Kav now. Anthony was a bit camp, but he's gone.

The three of us take a walk round the corner of the office to an Indian restaurant for lunch. I'm a bit nervous to eat but the second I enter the place my taste buds come alive. What about the garlic, though? I can't have garlic breath. *I definitely can't kiss the manager if that's the case. I wish we were staying overnight, just me and him, so we could have proper time together. I really must stop these thoughts.*

The menu has lots of dishes I've never heard of, so I order the chicken dopiaza, which I've had before with my Aunty Maria and Uncle Paul at the Indian restaurant near us. We would go there after Uncle Paul picked me and Aunty Maria up from Tuesday night WeightWatchers, which was one of the highlights of my week. I never lost any weight, but I loved spending time with Aunty Maria and Uncle Paul.

'Anything to drink? Indian beer?' asks the waiter.

Beer at 1pm?! I look at the other two – The Manager orders a large Bacardi and Coke, and Nick orders a *whole bottle* of wine 'for the table' he says to the waiter. *Considering I'm one of 'the table' I think this means I may be able to have some too. I like the sound of that! People actually drink alcohol at this hour of the day. What a life.*

I order a sparkling water.

CRAZY CHANCES

Summer passes, and apart from me doing my usual bits in the office, like making the tea and buying the staff sandwiches on the lunchtime run, I continue to spend most nights in my bedroom, at the new house, writing songs. I've also been in the *Daily Star* – there was a full-page interview about being The Manager's next big signing. 'Kavanagh QT – Music Boss Secret Weapon' was the headline. Me, a weapon! 'He has the looks of a film star, the personality of a magnet, and voice to send shivers down your spine,' writes Linda Duff, the seemingly mad-as-a-hatter Irish journalist. I did the interview when The Manager invited her to meet me at one of his agency parties in Manchester. 'Kavana is later this week set to be signed up by a major label in a deal worth £2 million,' it goes on. 'I can't believe it's me that's been picked, I have to keep pinching myself that it's all true. I'm having the time of my life. Having countless girls chasing me will be a dream come true,' I say. Apparently.

Mum takes it round the market and bingo in her handbag and shows anyone and everyone who will listen. I try to explain that some of the words aren't exactly true but she's not bothered. Her son is in the paper and I let her enjoy it.

Now I have real confirmation things are moving I feel less anxious, at least in the career department anyway. I'm also relieved that I don't look fat in the picture they use, which the photographer took on the night. I actually do look a bit handsome, if I may so myself! I also look happy without being too cheesy. Relaxed I'd say, which makes sense considering I'd had four glasses of free champagne by the time the picture was taken. Linda the journalist was helping herself to a few also, which may have added to the over-enthusiastic write-up. It feels natural doing interviews and having my picture taken, though. It feels right. The final words right underneath the picture are a bit much, though: 'BOY WONDER: Young newcomer Kavana has been groomed for pop stardom by top manager.' Sounds like I've been spending time in a beauty parlour, not working on becoming the next big pop star of the charts.

WANNABE MATES?

'As far as I know, Kavvy, it's just you and the Spice Girls performing and you're on first.'

It's now June, 1996 and I am officially a signed recording artist with a huge record deal with Virgin records! The other act that Ying who is now my official PA and looker after-er is talking about and who will also be performing at the Virgin Records HQ summer party alongside myself is a new pop group of five girls I keep hearing about who are also on the label, due to release their first single, a song called 'Wannabe'. The Manager got an early promo CD sent over and played it to me in the office a few weeks ago saying, 'It will never be a hit,' and that, 'Virgin are wasting their time.' I felt I had to agree to keep the peace but it's been stuck in my head ever since. I'm yet to meet the girls, but from what I've heard on the grapevine they are a force to be reckoned with and leave an impression wherever they go. It seems these girls have already done the rounds of all the magazines and are getting quite the reputation for being loud, in your face and a bit on the wild side. I'd recently been working on my album in the studio with a songwriter and producer called Eliot Kennedy, and Spice Girls, or 'Spice' as he was referring to them (I heard they'd only recently added the 'Girls' due to some American band already being called 'Spice'), were indeed something out of the ordinary.

'They are brilliant,' he kept saying. 'Mad, but brilliant. We've got this one song that's a smash, Kav; it's got a harmonica on it like bloody Stevie Wonder. And they can bloody write too!'

Blimey.

At the moment, and as far as the public are concerned, out of the two of us it's only me that has an inch of fame due to the release of my first single, 'Crazy Chance'. It made the top 40 chart (just about) after I popped up on various TV shows and in the pop mags to promote it. BBC's *Newsround* even came to Manchester where we filmed the video, which was bizarre. Not the filming of it but watching it on TV the week after. It's surreal watching a show that you've watched for years with a curry Pot Noodle on your knee (Fridays only), waiting for *Neighbours* to come on and seeing your own face on it. It hasn't been the chart-topping success my record label was hoping for but it's a start. Plus they have invested a lot of money in me, so we have to find a way of making it work with the next single.

'Does it need ironing?' Ying is holding up my pride and glory, my new pop-star uniform I have chosen and worn at various PAs and the odd TV show: a white Kappa tracksuit. This will be my attire for the Virgin conference gig as it feels comfortable while also standing out. It's basically a white suit, but Barry Manilow I am not. Oh no, I bought it in a cool shop in Camden for FIFTY pounds. I've never spent that much on an outfit in my life, but needs must if I want to stand out. In another dimension, 25 years in the future, Geri Halliwell will wear nothing *but* white, but today she is dressed in a skimpy blue boob tube with Frankenstein-looking 'Buffalo' boots, which seem to be everywhere at the moment. Geri and co. come bumbling into the huge garden area and join myself and Ying on the huge outdoor white plastic garden table under the gazebo in the currently empty 'party area' where we will perform tonight.

'Ellaaaaaw, sex-eh.'

I can tell a northern accent a mile off and before I can say 'eh up' in return, a gorgeous-looking girl approaches, all Neneh Cherry big curly corkscrew dark hair with highlights and light brown skin. She is beautiful, but wild like a lioness in silver leggings and a crop top. I go straight into 'cheeky chappy' mode, half wanting her to be my new friend and half wanting to flirt a bit. Although God forbid she catches on to the latter as she would no doubt eat me alive, and that's if I was straight. I remember thinking that I really had to be careful with how I play it meeting new pop pals – especially women – as although everyone loves a good flirt, it usually backfires when they misread me not wanting to take it any further than just friends as me not thinking they are attractive, which is NOT the case. I'm just terrified of them realising I'm gay. Maybe I'm overthinking. It's just that there's five girls against one closeted boy so it's a trickier ratio to keep up the jig. So much overthinking. Thing is, though, I doubt I'm Mel B's type anyway.

'Cool tattoo!' are the only words I can muster to this force of nature standing in front of me, referring to the Japanese writing to the side of her toned belly button. I really want to tell her how I love her hair but I think that would give the game away.

'Oh, cheers. 'Ave you got any?'

I begin to tell her about the green Irish shamrock on my arm that I had done recently – my first ever tattoo – but before I can offer up mine, hoping to bond us as new friends, she's off cackling to an assistant about stage times and when the food is coming. *Now that's a laugh and a half if ever I've heard one.* So I stand awkwardly, looking around at which girl to introduce myself to next.

It's times like this I'm glad I have Ying; I sometimes forget she basically works for me as we are more like best friends. I wish I could tell her about my feelings for The Manager and me having to put on this straight show and how it makes me sad. I wouldn't say I'm sad exactly, it's more a feeling of melancholy, like something's missing. Like, say, when you watch a film like *Watership Down*. Sad and happy at the same time. Happy sad. I've had it all my life but I thought that me becoming a pop star would take it away. It hasn't yet. There's no doubt the first single not charting in the top 10 has affected me but there's so much good stuff coming up, like the next video shoot in Spain and then supporting Boyzone on tour. I really need to shift my thinking to the good stuff.

The day rolls on and I slowly feel more comfortable in the company of my hopefully new friends. I'm going through my 'keeping a diary' phase, not wanting to forget a moment. It will actually only last all of three weeks and return again when I'm homeless and in my first rehab (spoiler alert), at which point it will be called a journal, but for now I go to bed pretty tipsy but fulfilled that not only did I somehow woo my new friends but that no one said a word about my sexuality! I'm so excited, I keep my diary entry simple with just one sentence to describe each girl of the soon-to-be-world-famous Spice Girls, including a percentage rating 'technique' that I'd made up to rate how good the day had been:

3rd June, 1997
An amazing day/night. Finally a 90 per cent!
I got to the meet the Spice Girls who were
LOVELY. They even cheered for me when I
sang, and we took pics together! Must not mix
Hooch alcopop with wine, though. Don't forget
to give Ying disposable camera back. I really
like the Spice Girls –

POP SCARS

Melanie B – Wild in a good way
Geri – Warm and clever and seems quite deep
Victoria – Seemed distracted and a bit quiet but
    lovely in the end and drank Pimm's
Mel C – Down to earth and funny
Emma – Cute, cheeky, and flirty (I think?!)

The room spins a bit as I reach for the bedside lamp. I'm so drunk I don't even hang up the Kappa tracksuit like Ying suggested so that it doesn't crease for tomorrow's Radio roadshow in Carlisle. I notice a light red stain on the trousers so drag myself up to clean it with my toothbrush and some soap. I give it a sniff. It's Pimm's.

FANDEMONIUM

Masturbating in the hotel shower before anyone comes knocking in the morning is always the best time to do it, I find. I'm usually too full after the hotel breakfast, and by the time we get back from whatever we're doing on any particular promo day I'm too tired for any form of self-pleasure. Shouldn't I be bedding every fan by now? I guess so but I don't fancy girls, and all my fans are girls. I love them and want to be their friend, but I just can't imagine doing the sex 'thing'. I don't think I'd have the heart to just use them anyway even if I *was* a straight Casanova type.

Myself, Ying and the new tour manager, Rob from Hull, are checking out of the Marriott in Swiss Cottage. Or rather, Ying is checking out while I loiter in the lobby and play with my phone. She's having some kind of issue at the front desk over room charges and I'm instantly on alert, moving closer to her in a full sweat as I realise I did in fact put my room number in the pay-per-view porn channel I stumbled across (searched for). I feel pretty mortified that Ying now has an image of me wanking off to porn like some hormonal Beavis and Butt-Head type as soon as I got in my room.

'Is this right, Kavvy? It says it's an adult channel.'

'Oh, erm, I think, maybe, oh I must have flicked on it by mistake.'

Why did I say 'flicked'?

'Oh' is the only word I can think of. 'Let's see the bill,' I say, like me asking to witness my own lie in black and white on hotel headed paper is going to make it better. The Danish-looking and definitely gay hotel receptionist looks at Ying and then twinkles his beady eyes to me. He probably knows I'm gay too and is wondering why I was watching straight porn in the first place.

'You entered your room number, sir – see, 206? It says at 11:34pm you chose the ADULT CHANNEL.'

OK, Bjorn, the all-seeing eye of Marriott Swiss Cottage. We get it. I watched porn! PORN! God forbid. Now please can you keep your whiny little voice down so the entire lobby doesn't know my late-night sins.

'It's fine, Ying,' I say, mustering back some authority, remembering that I have my KAV Ltd company business card. 'It's clearly a mistake but I'll put MY EXTRAS on my business card.'

The words come out of me as if I know what having a business card actually means, which I don't really. It feels good, though.

'It's not a problem; I just want to make sure they are charging you correctly, that's all.'

Ying probably doesn't care if I was watching porn as long as we can get it wrapped up and out of here.

We pay the bill and load up the stuff into the car that Rob has waiting for us in the hotel car park. An all-important under-18s nightclub in Kent beckons. I'm doing a few of these over the next month in preparation for the new single. It's a tried-and-tested formula apparently. The likes of Take That, Peter Andre and Boyzone had all done the rounds of the under-18s venues. So far, we've done two and I wasn't sure if the predominantly teenage-girl crowd wanted to beat me up or snog me. Memories of the girls at school, I guess. It's hard to tell. This is bound to be the hard bit, I suppose. I'm performing songs that they don't know yet after having only released one single.

'He was a bloody jobsworth!' Ying lightens the mood in the van, referring to the Dutch receptionist. She has a way to make me calm like no one else, it seems.

'Oh God, I know!' I play along. We don't need to mention the porn again, plus I won't be making the same mistake tonight.

I doubt there will be any late-night TV temptation in the Best Western, Maidstone.

* * *

The nightclub office smells like weed. I'm yet to venture into my spliff era so it doesn't really bother me and could also be mistaken for BO, but it's Rob that alerts our attention to it.

'Someone's had some wacky baccy in here,' he says,

almost a little too gossipy, possibly in an attempt to show his street cred (which has fallen flat since no one under the age of 60 uses the term 'wacky baccy'). But what our Rob lacks in 'cool' – which, let's face it, you don't really want or need when your job is to double up as both driver and security – he makes up for in not missing a trick, i.e. Rob is one very nosy man. Because I have no boundaries whatsoever and forget that work colleagues aren't necessarily friends, I forget that when I'm having private chats with Ying in the back of the van while going up and down whichever 'M' we are on, Rob is not in fact listening to drive-time traffic reports as his interested listening face suggests but he is in fact listening to every conversation we have. One example is me telling Ying that my Aunty Angela is newly single. Lo and behold the very next morning while making small talk at the services Rob coquettishly enquires, 'Who was at the Manchester gig again out of your lot? Your mam, sister – any uncles or aunties?' Meaning, 'Was your Aunty Angela, the attractive blonde at the PJ & Duncan after-show and if so when will I get to meet her now she's single?' Out of sheer boredom, Ying and I invented the 'Don't tell Rob' game where we would invent three short stories but make one of them so juicy that we just knew Rob wouldn't be able to contain himself in somehow repeating it to us at some point. It became a running joke and bonded us all on tour.

The now-infamous white Kappa tracksuit isn't an option for tonight's PA so I cobble together my other 'stage' option, which is a silver jeans, white vest and silver silk jacket combo recently brought back from the dead (the outfit, not PJ & Duncan) at the Deansgate dry cleaners and looking brand new. A dazzly number of sorts which if not rounded off with the white Adidas shell toes could be verging more on Bea Arthur on Broadway than Kavana in Kent. Anyway, back to the club. So the place is pretty packed for 9pm on a Wednesday, even if it is in the summer holidays. Anything with the number '18' in the title sounds ominous at the best of times, whether it's 'under', 'over' or 'rated', so I have no idea what to expect apart from the worst, and judging by the troublesome ready-to-attack faces on this lot I may just be right.

'Well, ladies. You're in for a treat tonight!' says the DJ over a booming mix of East 17's 'Thunder', which matches the current look on the front row of high-ponytailed faces.

'All the way from Manchester, he's the next big thing in pop and about to perform for you all. Give it up for KAVAAAAAARNA.'

I almost decide to reintroduce myself, pronouncing my name correctly, i.e. not rhyming with Banana, but it's too late. The jets of dry ice spurt out and the intro to my number-35 debut smash hit begins. In the words of Elvis, it's now or never. Although Radio City Music Hall, this is not. I swig a mouthful of now flat Diet Coke and make a bumbled sign of the cross, praying the holy spirit is indeed with me for the next 12 minutes and 57 seconds. In fact any spirit is welcome, ideally vodka, but there's strictly no drinking before gigs (plus it's a soft-drink bar).

'Go get 'em, Kavvy,' says Ying, as supportive as ever.

'That's if they don't get me first,' I half-jokingly reply.

Are gigs supposed to be this terrifying?

WHAT GOES ON TOUR...

Sheffield Arena, July, 1996

My first big arena tour. I am going to be one of the support acts for Irish boy band Boyzone, and things finally seem to be looking up. I've never played to such big audiences or had my very own – wait for it – stage set. The Manager has done some kind of a deal with Boyzone's crew where big wooden silver letters spelling out my name will be carried along with their rigs too. I'm on tour with other support acts including Peter Andre, who is now massive after his song 'Mysterious Girl' was released and is slowly becoming the song of the summer. Peter likes or chooses to keep himself to himself along with his dancers and security. There's also Sean Maguire from *EastEnders* who is now a solo pop singer – as well as being a right laugh and with an eye for the ladies – and a lovely girl singer from Birmingham with a belter of a voice called Rebekah Ryan whose record label MCA are pumping a lot of money into.

It's slowly starting to feel like I'm part of some kind of on-the-road pop family. I of course still have Ying by my side basically making sure all boxes are ticked in terms of our itinerary, where I need to be for soundchecks and whichever hotel we check into that night, and repeat. I'm a little tired but the overthinking seems to have subsided – it seems being busy is good for me. I need routine and structure like this, plus there's a big difference performing to a few thousand ready-made screaming Boyzone fans every night than an under-18s or a radio roadshow in Blackpool.

The Boyzone lads are exactly what I thought they would be so far: Irish. Which to me, and because they are from Dublin like my father and his Irish side of the family, means kind, humorous, warm, sensitive and of the deep-thinking variety. Each of them fills one of these roles in some sort of capacity. Ronan is of course the lead singer (ish), so he gets a pass to be a little more sure of himself, but so far he has been nothing but kind and friendly. Then there is Keith (pronounced 'Keet') who is right up my street – an open book and a whole lot of fun with a tendency to be one of the last in the bar after the show along with myself and Sean Maguire. If ever there was the 'craic' personified, Keet has it in buckets. Of Guinness. Then there is Shane, a hip-hop-styled gentle rogue of a man with a laid-back vibe about him. I find it particularly fascinating watching him sing 'Love Me For a Reason' while dressed as Warren G, but that's his thing and he stands by it. Mikey seems the more quiet one from all of the seven words we have so far exchanged: 1. Hey. 2. How. 3. Are. 4. You? 5. Good 6. Thanks. 7. You? He definitely seems to be the deep thinker or serious one. I wonder if he gets a bit sad at times like me? I of course could go straight to my usual fearful assumption of thinking Mikey knows I'm secretly gay and doesn't like me, but I don't because of the last but certainly not least member, Stephen, who I suspect or more to the point pray to all the beautiful gods in Irish heaven is gay.

This is not just some stupid teenage daydream wishful thinking. I mean, look – gaydar *is* a thing, OK? Most if not all gay people have it and it goes way beyond someone loving Kylie and quoting lines from *Hocus Pocus*. I've watched Stephen in interviews on TV and read what he says in the magazines, and apart from dodging the usual 'Have you got a girlfriend?' questions (answering, very much like myself, the statutory autopilot reply of 'I'm too busy for a relationship') or saying that he thinks Celine Dion is gorgeous (at least it's less obvious than my 'Madonna is sexy'), I just have a feeling about it. About him. It's certainly made being on tour a whole lot more exciting at the prospect that finally I'll be around someone I might actually be in with a chance with.

The first time our eyes meet properly is 4:46pm at Sheffield Arena. I know this because I pretended to look at the clock above the Coke machine by the door on the left near the kitchen.

A few of us were stood around talking, then suddenly he was there. Black cap, hoodie, baggy light blue jeans.

Sea-blue eyes with a smile that heals on the spot. No words spoken. Just feelings unlocked. A possible new future only an arm's length away.

Pure.

Soft.

Desire.

Joy.

Relief.

I am no longer camouflage.

BIG! TIME

This afternoon I am doing an interview and having some pictures taken for *Big!* magazine who are joining us on the Manchester leg of the tour to shoot it. Most of the mags are nice to me and lap up my cheeky northern banter, it's just disappointing to me that so far my favourite magazine of all and the one I've bought all my life – *Smash Hits* – hasn't been as forthcoming. Oh, to be on the cover of that one day. I still believe I will be, I just need to be patient. I had done one shoot with them already but I wasn't too happy with it. I wonder if they were actually laughing behind my back at what the concept was: me in a judge's wig and gown. Kavana QC to be exact, after the courtroom TV drama on ITV starring John Thaw. Being in fancy dress was not what I expected for my first appearance in my favourite magazine, let's just say.

BIG! have suggested taking some pics of me in soundcheck and backstage in my dressing room 'trying on' my stage outfit. Since this was casually mentioned by Ying this morning, I've not been able to concentrate. What did it mean? Me trying on the jacket? The trousers? Of course, it's the only day this week I've chosen to wear my new Calvin Klein slightly immodest briefs rather than normal boxers, so this could be an issue. Although saying that, I've been hammering the stairclimber at the gym as part of my pre-tour workout, so I'm fairly happy with my body at the moment. My legs don't look that skinny either. I'm also still sporting a tan from the all-inclusive Spanish holiday with Angela and Rob recently so . . .

We shoot some pics of me lumbering up and fake-rehearsing with a couple of my female dancers in the corridor then head to the seating part of the arena where I sit looking relaxed with feet dangling over the seats in front. A star is born at the Manchester G-MEX. Some more cheeky-chappy shots of me in the corridors, like me pointing to the STAGE THIS WAY sign and one of me outside my dressing room with my thumbs up to the KAVANA AND DANCERS sign before the dreaded question in waiting is then dropped.

'Can we do some shots of you trying your outfit on?'

Gulp.

'Er, yeah.'

Ying intervenes quick as lightning, knowing my fear of revealing too much skin (belly and upper arms basically) especially after The Manager's comments about my 'love handles'. Just because Peter Andre probably insists on being topless in every photo does not mean I'm anywhere near competing with that (I probably would, though, if I looked like him).

'Can we just do a shot in his clothes? It's not long before dinner and Kav needs a break before the show.'

'It's fine, Ying,' I say, and in a moment of absolute madness – and in order to distract *Big!* magazine from asking me to be shirtless – I start unbuttoning my jeans and drop them to my ankles without thinking, offering myself up like a stripper who turned up to the wrong hen party.

I stand to the side and tense my thigh in the hope that Tom, the now perplexed photographer, twigs that's my cue for him to start snapping, as surely he knows my right side underpants view is better with my right leg flexed?!

'Oh! Er . . . Sure!' chips in Gemma. 'I was going to suggest just opening your shirt a bit, but we can have you trying your trousers on if you don't mind us seeing your underpants instead . . .'

Ying passes me my silver stage trousers, leaving me now resigned to the fact my over-enthusiastic knee-jerk underpants-revealing reaction was avoidable, and that me actually posing looking like I'm trying them on may look more believable, rather than someone stood in the middle of the floor, jeans round ankles, looking like they've just got caught short running to the toilet mid shitting themselves.

'Here you go, Kavvy.'

Luckily time flies when you're mid exposing yourself for no reason, so a few more snaps of me changing the trousers and it's hugs all round while Ying escorts Gemma and Tom to the hospitality suite ready for tonight's gig.

I sign off: 'Maybe see you after the show at the hotel?'

Thank God that's over with. Hopefully I can redeem myself at the bar later.

'Oh well, at least we got some good shots in the arena. I love those ones of you in the seats,' comforts Ying, as we grab our AAA laminates to head to the catering.

'I hope they didn't think it was weird me pulling my trousers down like that. You couldn't see my willy, could you?' I ask, trusting I didn't give them more than they bargained for.

'Ha, don't be daft. I'm sure they've seen worse, Kavvy. Stop worrying!'

'Good,' I say, as we grab a tray and I notice the menu has a northern twist which provides me with me a cosy glow of feeling at home – just what I needed right now. Lancashire hotpot never looked so good. Just as I'm about to reach for the accompanying red cabbage I see the dessert chalk board menu: SPOTTED DICK AND CUSTARD and SHORTCRUST MANCHESTER TART. After the day I've had so far it feels quite apt really. I usually skip dessert anyway.

MAKE ME FEEL GOOD

London, winter, 1996

Although I'm a bit sad or, if I'm really honest, absolutely bereft that the tour has ended and I won't get to be in such close proximity to Stephen, nor my new friends who I'd just spent multiple hours a day with for weeks on end, I need to put my feelings to one side and focus on the big job at hand, and that means pulling out all the stops to make my third single a hit. I doubt Virgin will keep plugging money into me if I don't have one soon, and reading between the lines I could get dropped. Not all new artists get a hit straight away, though. Labelmates and good pals 911's first song only got to number 38 to my 35, but then their second one went to number 21 to my 26, and now their third single got to number 10. Not that I'm in any way obsessing over or comparing their chart positions, but it's the world I'm now in. And it means that if I am to follow form to my cheeky pop pals then I should ideally be next to have that bigger hit. Third time lucky, as they say.

We shoot the third video for my next single, a cover of Shalamar's eighties soul classic 'I Can Make You Feel Good'. It's chosen by my ever-patient and lovely A&R woman Joanne and demoed by yours truly in my bedroom on my Fostex 4-Track before being sent to top producers Absolute to give it a once-over. I'm in a café-cum-bar in North London and my female love interest is none other than the girl from the Boddingtons advert, Melanie Sykes. When Melanie rocks up, all laid-back northern and cool as a cucumber, I feel like she could eat me alive (or possibly be my hot older sister) rather than someone I'm about to seduce in a café, lip-syncing to an eighties soul classic in my denim jacket and unruly centre parting (Shockwaves hair wax is a no-no for hair longer than a crew cut, it seems). It's also freezing. Like proper 'Puff the Magic Dragon smoke rings blowing out of mouth' cold. Less of the puff today, though. Apart from the copious cigs me and Melanie are smoking while getting on like a house on fire.

Melanie couldn't be more easy to work with, or should I say, sing at. It's me that's embarrassed not her. I really need to take charge. The director keeps saying, 'Let's see you flirt a bit, come on!' I think I'm flirting so I'm not sure what else he means. Melanie is stunning – gay or not, it's obvious. I just hope she doesn't think I'm acting like a bloody weirdo. Today's a big deal. It's also the first video shoot where I've had a proper catering van for all the crew. Eat to the Beat they are called, and it's delicious. I'm trying to watch the calories – or more to the point watch any type of food that may cause unnecessary bloating, being cautious of my stomach even though I didn't eat much last night and when I woke up this morning my stomach was flatter than normal. *I could always try the making-myself-sick thing?* I've done it a few times but last time my eyes were so red and watery after I came back from sneaking off to do it that my make-up artist asked if I'd been crying.

But things are looking positive. More press, radio and TV promo ensues. We find out that Radio 1 have added 'I Can Make You Feel Good' to their A-list, which means it's getting lots of airplay. This is a huge change as my last two singles have had none apart from the odd regional radio playlist. I don't want to get my hopes up too much but it's looking like out of all of them so far this song has the best shot yet at getting in the top 20 at least. Even Woolworths have forecast it to be number 15. *Eek.* What also helps is that ICMUFG is being released in the first week of January – a good time for those in the know to put out a song apparently.

I'm smoking a cigarette in the garden of the new little house I bought for me and Mum and Dad. A few days off while we wait to hear the midweek chart, which happens to be today, Wednesday. I've been so consumed by the chart position that by now I'm mentally exhausted and have convinced myself it's not done well, which also means my life is now over. I can hear my dad's little radio which he takes with him while pottering around the house. He always needs music. Mum is still getting her head around the portable phone we've had installed. No wires. She uses it like a walkie-talkie and keeps forgetting to put it back on the base downstairs after she's done chatting to whichever family member she's been on the phone to, or the doctor asking for more co-codamol after she's run out. I distract myself by feeding Mickey, my new cat. I bought him on Boxing Day from a random pet shop in Bury. Mickey is a wild little thing and the complete opposite of Arnold, who it turned out didn't just have a tummy bug but was very ill indeed and he quickly died of the cat version of AIDS. It's a weirdly bittersweet memory, though, because it was The Manager who took me to and from the vet's and paid for all of Arnold's care and bills. I miss those days. Not Arnold being sick, obviously – I'm talking about the days when it was just The Manager and I, when we spent more time together and it felt like he was my protector and mentor and my everything, I guess. Fast forward to almost two years later and I hardly see him. I simply don't have time to go into the office when he's there, and every decision made is passed on to me through Ying or the record label. I attempted to make a few appointments with him but he was either busy or 'not in today'. I also heard he's been seen with a couple of other guys, a new up-and-coming act for his label. Huh?! How can he even think of focusing on anyone else but me after *everything* we have been through together?

Because I bought this house outright there is no

mortgage, so it's only the other bills my parents have to pay for. It's actually a lot smaller than the council house, so it means Mum and Dad have fewer bills. Anyway, with the success of the tour I've got so much money, more than I ever thought I would see in my entire life, I just help with whatever's needed as and when.

'Anthoneeeeeeee, it's Ying on the phone.'

Mum is yelling from the bathroom which means the phone is not downstairs on its rightful place on the stand with the plastic flowers and the *Yellow Pages*. Which also means there's a chance it could run out mid-conversation with Ying who has likely gone into the office on our one day off from promoting the single and has heard what the midweek is. Which also means it could cut off just as she's telling me the bad news. Which also means if it does cut off right after she says, 'Hi, darling, I have the midweek. It's . . .'

I'll have to try not to faint and run back downstairs to put the handset back on the charger for two minutes to give it enough battery power to find out and then call back . . . but then she could call my mobile phone? *Why didn't she call my mobile phone?!*

'Anthonyyyyyyyyyy. YING!'

My mum has that bewildered panic in her voice which she gets at times for no reason at all, unless her psychic powers are telling her this is urgent, which of course it is to me, but Mum doesn't know today is the midweek, unless she's been earwigging.

I run up the stairs and, breathless, I grab the phone from Mum who is stood holding it by the bathroom sink with a look of pre-emptive shock in a cloud of Insette hairspray and Elizabeth Taylor's White Diamonds copy perfume off the market, in the hope that either the battery doesn't run out or that her son's life, career and livelihood aren't about to go down the (bathroom) drain.

'Hello?' I gasp, half from being out of breath from running up the stairs, half from the terror of hearing news that could ruin everything

'Hi, Kavvy. So . . . we've just got the midweek . . .'

Our Father, Who art in heaven,

'It's . . .'

Hallowed be thy name,

'Number . . .'

Thy Kingdom come; thy will be done,

'EIGHT.'

On earth as it is in . . .

'What?! You're fucking joking, right?! Jesus-fucking-Christ. EIGHT?!'

I do hope Our Father's will is that he doesn't mind me swearing in response to his almighty life-changing lottery-of-the-pop-charts miracle

'Woooohoo!! Oh my GOD, Ying. I can't believe it. Will it stay there? Will it go higher? What if it falls lower?!'

'Congratulations, Kavvy. You deserve it. You've worked so hard for this. Enjoy the moment!'

'Oh, wow. Ying! I couldn't have done this without you. WE couldn't have done this without . . . er, you. I mean, well, er, you know what I mean!'

My sincerity is not lost on Ying. She knows me well enough to know how much I appreciate her.

'Stop bloody swearin',' Mum yells from the bedroom. There must be a delay.

'I'm not swearing anymore. It's gone in at number eight, Mum!'

'Oh, that's good 'nt it?'

I can hear the phones ringing and the background chatter in the office while Ying holds on the other end of the line.

'I'll let you go, Kavvy. We're getting some requests for you, and Virgin are on the case with *Top of the Pops* now we know the good news, so fingers crossed we get a performance on next week's show. I'll call you later with updates and next week's itinerary.'

Christ. Top of the Pops. *Now it's really becoming real. What will I wear? I'll need to rehearse. Will I sing live?*

'Have you seen my teeth anywhere?'

Mum has other things on her mind if she wants to make the next bus to Kwik Save.

'You was in the bathroom last, have a look in there,' I tell her, while the prospect of finally having my first top 10 hit and making an appearance on my lifelong favourite TV show starts to really sink in.

LIKE A VIRGIN

My record label Virgin have invited me to sit on their top table at this year's BRIT Awards. The BRIT Awards! I have never been to an awards show before and can hardly contain my excitement. Ying tells me that only artists and record company people are allowed at the table. This means that:

1. They think I'm going to be a big star.
2. There will be free drinks flowing.
3. I won't have her watching over me as usual.

I hope that doesn't sound mean, but it does feel exciting. Ying told me that she has been given strict orders for me not to drink too much or go to any after-parties as I have my first ever *Smash Hits* cover shoot in the morning. *Smash Hits,* my dream. So the timing could really not be worse for an unchaperoned night of freedom.

This was also the very same BRITS where my new labelmates the Spice Girls were about to sweep the board and make headlines all over the world with Ginger Spice's Union Jack dress, *and* Prince was rumoured to be performing.

I am staying at the Royal Garden Hotel on Kensington High Street. The stylist has biked over a huge bag of designer clothes which I must go through and choose my outfit from for the night. It seems that now I've finally had my first top 10 single Virgin are pushing the boat out a bit more, and along with appointing my own hairdresser, which seems extravagant considering I have curtains and can do it myself, a fashion stylist is what all newly established pop stars like me must also have, apparently. Ying, as always, is on the ball with my timekeeping:

'Make sure you're down in reception for 6:30pm, Kavvy. OK?'

'That seems a bit early? It doesn't start until 8pm.'

The hotel lift arrives and I practically jump in as the doors close, with Ying's final words ringing in my ears.

'6:30pm is the time our car is booked for and there will be press for the red carpet, so choose something nice.'

I press the button for the sixth floor and huddle in with some other music types and two women in burkas with Harrods bags. The doors close and the thinking starts . . .

Wear something nice. Nice? I don't want nice. I want sexy, cool and dramatic. Nice is what Boyzone wear.

They're lovely guys but all that cream and white is just not me. Oh God, what will I wear? I hope everything fits. Where's my hairdresser? Does he think I'm gay? Is he gay and if he is, why doesn't he say? Are you supposed to say? I wish gay people wore a badge so I'd know who I could have a chance with. I feel fat. Am I fat? Will there be a minibar in my room? I hope it's not locked. I should eat something. I'm too nervous to eat something. I'll have a small wine or two or maybe a Diet Coke with one of those mini gins. I was sick on gin once in Cornwall, though. OK, I won't have anything. I wonder if Ying knows I'm gay? OMG Mel C will be there. What if she saw me say I fancy her in Smash Hits? *What if she fancies me? She's gorgeous and I do like her but not like that. We could date and I could keep making excuses re the sex part. That's not fair on her though, is it? Am I gay? I love girls but I fancy boys. I need a drink.*

The lift doors open on my floor and I head to the room. My rambling thoughts subside and I am aware that I may have been a bit rude to Ying by not getting in the lift with her. I wish I didn't feel so guilty about things all the time. Maybe Catholic guilt is a real thing after all. I used to make things up when going to confession after church on a Sunday with my mum. I couldn't think of anything I'd done wrong, so in fact I was telling lies while doing the very thing that's supposed to give me forgiveness:

'Bless me, Father, for I have sinned. My last confession was last Sunday and on Wednesday, I pushed in the school dinner queue in front of Alison Jones when she wasn't looking. I also stole 20p from my mum's purse when she was talking to the next-door neighbour. This is all I can remember. I am sorry for these and all my sins.'

Father Bergin, the local priest, would usually be the one who would assign me a penance, taking into account what I'd done, which would be a prayer or sometimes a number of prayers. I would always wonder why sometimes it would be 'Hail Marys' and other times 'Our Fathers'. I decided that the 'Our Fathers' were for the worse things I'd supposedly done, as one time the only sin I could think of was that I'd forgotten to feed Arnold (another lie because my dad fed him every day) and I got one 'Hail Mary' instead of the three 'Our Fathers' and two 'Hail Marys' I got for the purse episode.

At the end of my confessions I would have to say the 'Prayer of the Penitent', which was also known as the 'Act of Contrition'. I grew to savour saying this one because to my surprise, after it feeling like such a burden to do and emphasised what a bad person I was, I realised that Madonna had a whole song on her new album *Like a Prayer* named the very same. I would join my hands in prayer and, already kneeling, close my eyes and imagine myself in the pop video and would escape into the theatrics of it all . . .

'My God, I am sorry for my sins with *all* (I would emphasise the 'all' for extra drama) my heart. In choosing to do wrong and failing to do good, I have sinned against you whom I should love above all things. I firmly intend, with your help, to do penance, to sin no more (Jesus, all this for a dinner queue) and to avoid *whatever* (said earnestly in possible whisper depending if it was Father Allan, the other priest who had a hearing aid) leads me to sin. Our saviour Jesus Christ suffered and died for us. In his name, my God, have mercy.'

I would then receive absolution from God via the priest, which would give me pardon and peace from my sins and I'd be sent out to fulfil my act of penance which, depending on how many prayers he'd given me, would either be done there and then on a bench in the church or have to wait until we got home as Mother had afternoon bingo on a Sunday and she wasn't missing that for any god.

I'm too sensitive. Sometimes when Ying and I talk I can see sadness in her eyes. I know the look because I see it in my mother's eyes too. Is it because they are sad themselves or that they are sad for *me*? Can they tell I'm hiding this big gay secret and that I'm lonely sometimes? Oh God, I hope not. I wonder what it must be like for Ying having to be running around after me and then watch me get all the praise. Who looks after her? She has become my best friend, I guess. After all, she has been with me non-stop for the last 12 months. We have a lot of fun on our travels, but the long radio tours up and down the country and the dodgy under-18s nightclubs where some fans accuse her of being my girlfriend and call her a 'Chinese bitch' must be tough, but she doesn't say anything to me about it. I guess she has to keep a professional line as it's her job to look after me and make sure everything runs smoothly.

I swipe the key in the door and see I have been put in a suite. There is a huge white bed and a massive view over Kensington Gardens, which even in the dark looks stunning. I see on the dresser there is a silver bucket with a bottle of champagne and a note:

TO KAVANA, WITH COMPLIMENTS OF VIRGIN RECORDS.

So much for not drinking too much. They clearly didn't get the memo.

It feels like I have truly arrived. This is like something out of a movie, or at least this is *my* movie and I am literally living in a world I've only dreamed of. I've never actually opened a bottle of champagne before and I'm afraid of it exploding, so I decide to check the minibar which, to my relief, is unlocked and full of every mini alcoholic drink and mixer I can think of. I settle on two mini Smirnoffs and an icy cold Diet Coke. I pour in the vodka and mix in the Coke and the bubbles pop and fizz in my face. I love the smell of vodka. It's so clean smelling but so strong too. I overheard Uncle Donald say to my dad once at one of the family dos that it's the 'only drink that you can't smell on your breath'. But I'm not so sure because Uncle Donald always smells like booze so he was either wrong or didn't drink vodka. Either way, it was fine for me as I have my new Jean Paul Gaultier cologne which will disguise any evidence of alcohol, plus I'm only young and my mum said Uncle Donald's had a drinking problem for years and is probably an alcoholic and that's why his second wife divorced him so no wonder he reeks of it.

I take a big swig, then a second and a third. Within moments I get a warm rush in my stomach which then rises to my head and suddenly any and every niggling worry I have in the world disappears. I feel like a kid in a candy store here in this grand hotel room with as much of this magic confidence-boosting relaxing elixir as I want. *This works. This really works. But I must not have too much.* Not yet anyway, as there could be traffic on the way to the show and I always start to feel uncomfortable, edgy almost, when the buzz starts to wear off, so I'll need to have just have enough to keep me going until I get there and can have more.

The phone rings and jolts me out of my warm haze. It's Ying.

'Thirty minutes to go, Kavvy. Did you choose your outfit?'

'Sure did. Wait till you see it, you're going to love . . .'

'Shall I come over and help you? I'll come on up.'

I haven't even looked in the bag of clothes. *How on earth have I been in this room for so long already?*

'Well, if you want to you can. Although I can dress myse—'

'See you in a min!'

It's not so much the not-being-ready-on-time I'm bothered about, it's the fact I've not finished my drink and need to find a place to hide the mini bottles of vodka, which is something I'll have down to a fine art one day when having a drink becomes as important to me as oxygen. I slam the rest of the drink in one go, letting out a big boozy burp, and shove the miniatures under one of the huge pillows. *She won't see them under there.* She knocks and I let her in.

'Bloody hell, it stinks in here! How come you're not dressed? And you might want to ease up on the aftershave.'

I'd spritzed myself just in case she could smell the vodka.

'It's not aftershave, it's cologne. I was just trying it out. Does it smell a bit girly? Here. Look at these cool jeans,' I say to distract her.

We both dive into the clothes and after her suggesting the skull-and-cross T-shirt might be a bit much for my first red carpet, we settle on a Benetton black-and-white jumper and white Helmut Lang jeans. The hairdresser swings by and makes my curtains neater with a hairdryer and wax and I'm good to go.

Virgin have sent us a car with blacked-out windows. I usually feel a bit embarrassed when the driver insists on opening the door for me and so always let Ying in first, but not tonight. Maybe it's the vodka but I'm feeling super-confident and jump in first without thanking him. The driver's in a chirpy mood though, thankfully.

'Busy one tonight. I've been told to wait for you afterwards to take you to the Spice Girls' private party.'

My heart skips a beat. Private party? Spice Girls?

'Oh, right!' I reply, trying to contain the excitement in my voice.

Ying seems apprehensive and makes a quick call while I envision myself partying with the biggest stars in town tonight.

'Yes, I see. It's at Quo Vadis?' she says.

'Are we invited then?!' I beg, I mean, ask.

'Yeah, they're keeping it hush-hush. It's just for the Virgin Records lot.'

I'm so glad I'm with Virgin Records. Now they have all this success with the Spice Girls I'm bound to be their next priority. Maybe I'll crack America too. God, I feel good.

Our driver sets off and about 10 minutes in we hit traffic. A lot of traffic. Now I see why Ying was right. Thankfully, the traffic starts to move again and even though this is possibly set to be the most exciting night of my life, all I can think about is getting another drink. *It must be vodka that does that to me. I'll be switching to wine when I get to the table. Wine is more civilised anyway and I can sip it.*

Finally, we arrive at the venue and it's crazy busy. Ying gets out first to talk some PR guy while I wait in the back of the car, and suddenly my stomach is in knots with nerves and adrenaline. There's a big long barrier with fans behind it and they are shouting the names of the celebrities that are getting their photo taken on the red carpet. *Click-flash, click-flash.* I see a slim guy in a huge hat smiling and waving to the crowd and realise it's Jay Kay from Jamiroquai. Then the singer from Skunk Anansie arrives, I think she's called Skin and she looks terrifying but beautiful at the same time. The paparazzi are going nuts at someone who's just arrived but all I can see is silver sparkles and big, big hair. Holy shit, it's Diana Ross. I wonder where Prince or

'The Artist' as he's now known as is. I am literally speechless and wish I was in a boy band or a group so I didn't have to do this by myself. Ying comes back to the car and the driver gets out to open my door. It's my turn to walk the carpet and get my picture taken. *What if the paparazzi don't know who I am? What if the fans who are screaming don't scream or shout my name? I NEED A DRINK!*

'Come on now, Kavvy. It's your turn. Don't worry, you look great. Just stand and smile for a few seconds and walk to the other side where I'll be waiting.'

I take a deep breath and wait at the barrier for a manic woman with a headset and clipboard to signal me in. She gives me the go-ahead and I walk onto the area where the red carpet is. *Click-flash, click-flash.* What seemed like a few photographers from the car window is now a sea of them, frantic and shouting in front of me.

'Over here, Kavana.'

They do know who I am!

'This way, mate.'

'Kavana, over to your left. That's it. A few more.'

The crowd have spotted me too and a chubby girl with red hair is screaming:

'Kavana! Oh my God, it's Kavana!'

I bite my lip to stop it trembling and give a thumbs up to her and smile.

I am both terrified and ecstatic, but most of all I am relieved. Reassured that I am finally a bona fide pop star and I'm exactly where I'm meant to be.

BRIT AWARDS – PART TWO

Inside the venue I am ushered in by another frantic person wearing a headset to the table I will be joining – that of the record companies. It appears Virgin have a whole area where some of the chosen artists and execs will be sitting. Organised mayhem. Copious amounts of booze on each table along with the finest silverware and tablecloths and ashtrays. Marlboro Lights and vodka, Veuve Clicquot, red and white wines. Untouched bottles of mineral water. I hover nervously at the table until I'm beckoned to sit down by a goth androgynous-looking human with pasty white skin and eyeliner. *Way too cool a person to be offering me up a place at the pop awards banquet*, I think, but I accept and plonk down next to him anyway. He's American or could be Canadian, I'm not sure. I immediately feel relaxed with him, though, and his what may also be southern drawl.

'Oh, heeey, you're Kavaaaarna?' he asks, a bit nasally but with warmth and mischief in his eyes. And before I can say, 'Yes, I'm completely out of my depth here, please talk to me and don't leave my side all night,' I twig that he is in fact Brian Molko from the indie alt-rock band Placebo. *What the actual fuck?* Well, of course it makes sense now – Virgin Records have a huge roster of eclectic bands and artistes! How very punk of them to place a teen pop star next to someone who looks like a member of the Addams Family with a Lou Reed coolness to boot. Maybe I can drop in that *Transformer* changed my life . . . well, it hasn't yet, but I know it did my sister's and I understand the aesthetic.

My coolness now feels multiplied as I reach for the champagne from one of the buckets on the table and somehow muster the confidence to pour myself a glass, offering my new friend Brian a top-up also. Ray Cooper, the label boss and the man who signed me is facing me and gives me his big jolly grin and a thumbs up. *Thank God I've finally had a hit, it would be awkward to say the least if I was sitting at the table with a third flop under my belt after the advance I've banked from them and the money they've so far spent on little old me,* I think. *Although, saying that, if that was the case I'd probably be in the cheap seats rather than one of the top tables.* I read in the NME that Brian is a 'no fucks given bisexual', so that adds to my not having to act too straight in his company, although this now very well cemented persona I have become is so second nature to me I forget what the real gay version of me actually is.

Suddenly I'm distracted by a ruckus as a man in leather trousers has arrived and is swaying around our table, and Ray in particular.

He's just 'flown in from New York' apparently, according to what I think he just said or shouted at the top of his voice, champagne glass sloshing in hand, while smothering those he is familiar with on our table with kisses and what seems to be a lap dance for Ray. On closer inspection I realise it's Simon Le Bon. There's another wild-eyed American-sounding guy who has also plonked himself at the table and who's openly produced a see-through plastic tube of what looks like pink pills of some sort and is passing them round the table. 'Oh, honey, she's fucked,' says Brian, non-plussed, rolling his eyes, having probably seen it all before. 'What are these?' I ask innocently, as I somehow get passed the tube of mystery drugs. *Most likely E, I think, or if they're from New York, could be some kind of Quaalude.* Seeing as this isn't Studio 54 nor is it the 1970s it's most likely the former.

'Be careful, Kavanaaaa,' warns Brian. At least he's taken out the 'r' now. 'They look like pink Ecstasy pills and super-strong – you gotta be careful, OK?'

I take a better look at the tube under the table so no one else sees my inspection apart from Brian. Not that it matters what they look like. *They all do the same job, plus I could just take half and see how I go . . .* I'm all too aware I have the cover shoot in the morning, but I've got the hunger for it now. *Imagine how much better this night could get with a bit of Ecstasy sprinkled in the mix?* I bite half off and swig the rest of my champagne, shoving the other half into the tighter little pocket in my Helmut Lang jeans. No going back now.

* * *

'Charlie, are you out there somewhere, Charlie,' asks Mrs Merton, aka comedian Caroline Aherne who is onstage about to present an award. 'Only everyone backstage is looking for you.'

Brilliant. Trust a northerner. The award in question is for Best British Single and rumour has it that it may well end up going to five girls who are sat on the next table to me, and who also brought the house down at the start of the night by performing their new single 'Who Do You Think You Are'.

'And the winners of Best British Single . . . We've seen these brazen hussies earlier, the little Spice Girls!'

Earls Court erupts in mainly happy cheers, as does our Virgin table and the not-now-so-little (certainly in the fame and success department) Spice Girls who get up one by one to make their way to the stage to collect their award. We all sit clapping, cheering and possibly gurning, and I clap like a happy seal, genuinely feeling joy and pride for my labelmates. I think I catch the eye of Emma who is dazzling in a silver dress and diamanté tiara and I think she smiles, acknowledging me as if to say, 'OMG, hey, Kav!' At least in my head anyway. The other four, who have also changed into couture dresses, float past the table on their way to the stage to pick up the award. Walking successes, loyalty and girl power. I think of the time we were in a field under a gazebo waiting to perform at the Virgin Conference.

That now more familiar warm rush of narcotic euphoria has arrived, quelling every nerve and flushing my system with sheer pleasure. I think the absolute joy and excitement of witnessing the colourful explosion and rapturous applause of the girls has made my little pink helper start to kick in also. *Oh God.*

I down the glass of white wine in front of me. It seems to have been poured for me by one of the waiters while I was too busy hoping one of the girls would see me cheering for them. *I really must pace myself. I cannot be hungover for the* Smash Hits *shoot tomorrow, especially since new editor Gav has hinted it's for the cover and there is no way I can fuck that up, BRIT Awards or not. I've already had quite a bit, I should probably stop and stick to the water. I need to stand up and move.* It's kicking in more and I need to talk, laugh, love! I feel so much love and stability I could give a speech on the beauty and texture of the granary cob roll I'm yet to touch on the side plate next to me.

I just want to connect.

I want to feel this way forever.

This is who I really am.

I pop the other half.

COVER BOY

Note to self: never take drugs off a stranger, at an awards show, the night before you have a photo shoot for the front cover of a magazine. Not just any magazine either, we are talking *the* magazine you've waited most of your life to be on the cover of. That one.

Second note to self: if you do take said drug from stranger, do not under any circumstances decide it's a good idea mid-peak of it taking effect to approach another more successful and sane pop star (in this case the lovely singer Louise from Eternal) declaring your undying love and that you and her should record a duet and be 'the next Kylie and Jason'. I may or may not have also complimented her on how amazing her hair looked. *Help.*

The joys of the morning after, though, and oh what a night it was! Apart from the madness of the BRITS itself, the night carried on until the early hours at the private after-party that Virgin did in fact throw for the Spice Girls just as the driver said would happen. By that point, and because of my antics so far that evening, it's all a bit sketchy. I do remember being at the after-party but it was so dark and packed full of people, plus I know Ying was watching the clock (i.e. doing her job) so it was hard to really relax into it. I definitely remember trying to order the grilled club sandwich in my altered state from the room service menu back at my hotel room at 1:30am, a heavy and possibly indigestible choice at such a time, but they were out and the only other choices were spaghetti bolognaise or the Arabic meze platter (including cauliflower – odd choices for a late-night menu, it seems) so I didn't bother.

Today we will be trying something new. I shall be showing my whole chest, including nipples. The new editor of *Smash Hits,* Gav, is unlike any other magazine editor I've met so far. He oozes enthusiasm, charm and is so down to earth and just one big ball of laid-back fun. He's also very handsome in a shabby indie wholesome cool way. He's not gay, though. He also doesn't push me on anything too personal when we meet. I just think he genuinely loves his job and wants to take *Smash Hits* back to what it was before the last editor came on board, who I think tried to make it a bit too cool for school. It was her first time as an editor, though, and good luck to her – even if she did dress me up in a wig and cloak for the only shoot she let me do. But times have changed and I am grateful for any support so far. Back to the nipples. So the idea is that I will pull my shirt open and on my bare chest in big colourful letters will be the word 'Star'. I mean, if you say so. I've waited to be on the cover of *Smash Hits* for as long as I can remember, so they can write 'Twat' for all I care.

Editor Gav is having a nosy at the morning papers that have landed in the studio along with the coffee and the pastries. *No, thanks.* I could just about manage a banana and am having trouble keeping that down. There's a pic in the *Daily Star* of Mel C at last night's party looking less Sporty Spice and more Superstar Stylish Spice in her sexy brown sheer fitted dress. Gav plays along with the rumour that I fancy Mel, as I said it in the magazine not too long ago. Mel C is also Gav's fave too, so we play-fight who's going to win the hand of the sporty one. If only he knew . . .

We go for a different hairstyle for my first cover. The centre parting was definitely a look at first but now it seems every pop boy has one. It's either that or those carefully styled spikes that seem like an absolute mission to maintain. The style we are going for today is bit more messy, more of a fringe, and makes me look a bit more *avant-garde*. It will need maintenance, though – if it goes too flat on my head I'll either look like a young schoolboy or, with my face, Janette Krankie. Gav whacks on some music to get us in the mood and I do my pop-star poses as per, but I'm feeling happy and secure in my role now and, knowing I'm getting the cover, I relax a bit and have some fun with it.

I'm told that there's a new American boy band in the photo studio below us who have asked to meet me. They are called *NSYNC and are apparently fans of my music. I suddenly feel rejuvenated that not only have a band from the US of A even heard of me, but they are fans? Surely not?! I've seen those guys in a couple of magazines and they don't look the type that would admit to liking someone like me; then again, I know they can really sing and maybe they can see through all the image stuff and appreciate my voice too?

'Sure thing. I'd love to meet them! Gimme five mins to change,' I say, wondering why I am also now apparently American.

I grab a face wipe from the make-up artist and frantically wipe off the layers of foundation and powder that have accumulated on my face as the morning's shoot has gone on. I don't want to look too camp for these guys. Because of my long eyelashes any make-up at all makes me look extra girly, so it's a constant thing in my head to be mindful of. I once cut them off when I was 10 years old, blaming it on me getting too close to the electric fire in our living room while playing tiddlywinks. No idea why I used that excuse either, as the fire had bars on it and I'd never actually played tiddlywinks in my life.

I decide the rainbow zigzagged silk shirt I've had on also has to go. It did the trick for the shoot with me pulling it open to reveal my bare chest, but up close and personal it's a bit much. I shove on the Maharishi hoodie I was wearing beforehand which conveniently is army green. *Ta-da!* Butches me up in seconds.

Five fresh-looking guys saunter in one by one.

'I'm Justin,' says boy-band member number one

with a Colgate-white smile and SUN-IN looking high-lighted hair. 'It's so great to meet you. We love your music, man.'

Man? Yikes, just as well I got rid of the shirt. I better get my cool on. Before I can say, 'Gee, thanks y'all,' I go in for the handshake-cum-hug. I feel Justin's warm-toned chest against mine. It feels good, and for a few seconds a spark of desire washes over me. I push it out of my mind and go straight (pardon the pun) to the next member of the band who is also standing in line, making me feel a bit like the Queen at the Royal Variety Performance.

'I'm Joey.' This guy's a bit more goofy, for want of a better word, but still very sweet, as are the others who I say hello to one by one. *It's nice to feel like a bit of a star,* I think. *I'm not sure how the UK will take to this lot but I hear they are massive in Germany, so if they don't have much luck here or back in America then they could always make a career out there with it being one of the biggest markets.*

I always wonder how it must be doing all that touring as a group rather than just by yourself. How do they decide who says what in each interview? There is no doubt it's exhausting doing all this by myself and having to be 'on' for every new journalist or radio presenter or TV host I meet but I think it's best this way, or at least for me it is. On the other hand, it would certainly seem easier knowing you have someone else to back you up. My sexuality would still be a concern, though. The pressure of being around three or four other straight boy-band members would be a lot. They would have to either be in on the secret and protect it or you'd be having to keep up the pretence in front of them as well, and you'd never feel relaxed. *Well, I've made my bed so I've just got to lie in it.*

SPIRALS AND CARPETS

Weekend off from promo and best friend Andrew is up from Leeds University where he's now studying. Not only that but he's having a gathering at his Aunty Doreen's family home while he house-sits. Seeing my oldest pal always takes me straight back to being 12 years old again when we were just two lost souls who found solace in each other's quirky ways and music taste. Andrew is still in his indie era but now name-checks bands like Belle and Sebastian and Pulp rather than The Smiths like he used to, whereas I'm going through my neo-soul Erykah Badu and Maxwell phase.

Andrew and I were neighbours but never went to the same school. We were the type of best friends who saw each other the odd school night but mainly at the weekends, where us two hormonal teenagers would enjoy Saturday afternoons watching VHS recordings of late-night Australian cult show *Prisoner: Cell Block H* with tea and buttered crumpets and the curtains drawn.

Most other lads our age would be down the shopping centre meeting girls or playing football, but not us two. Our other weekend activity when not bingeing on low-budget female-led prison dramas was making tape recordings of our very own episodes of *Neighbours* where I would play battleaxe Mrs Mangel to his Plain-Jane-Superbrain character or the posh old grandmother Helen Daniels, depending on where the made-up-on-the-spot episode took us. Like any soap opera, the climax or cliffhanger of our sometimes-up-to-20-minutes cassette-tape recordings would always end with my character Mrs Mangel doing something terrible to whoever Andrew was playing, which was usually the more pitiful role to add contrast and heightened drama. One of my favourite improvised pieces was when Helen Daniels (Andrew) was pushed down the stairs of her own house by a terrifying Mrs Mangel (me) over an evil plot to kidnap Bouncer the loveable labrador. To add extra drama and sorrow we decided that Mrs Daniels was on this occasion paralysed and in a wheelchair. Considering we were both still closeted teenagers who bizarrely didn't tell each other until years later and hadn't even heard of Bette Davis or Joan Crawford apart from in Madonna's 'Vogue' rap, it was all bit Baby Jane in hindsight. Who said geeks weren't ahead of their time?

Back to the housewarming at Aunty Doreen's . . . My actual school friend Matt was invited along with Andrew's new college pals, so Matt and I decide to go into town before the party to have a few drinks and warm up for the occasion. We decide to go to the very club where it all started, as it's easy to get into and there's never any trouble. I also have ulterior motives. I want to score some stuff to perk the party up – it seems no night out is now worth it for me without a bit of coke or the odd E these days. We say to ourselves that we can't get to the party later than 10-ish otherwise it will look bad and not fair on Andrew who has already texted to say there's 'plenty of beers and cider, don't worry,' and, 'don't be turning up late and wasted'. *He knows me too well. Knowing him, though, those beers will be the 3 per cent volume German beers he tried to palm me off with at Christmas that don't even touch the sides, so we will have to do a stop at the off-licence in the taxi on the way there too.*

Inside the club the music is pumping as usual, but it's early so it's not even full yet. I scope out the dance floor looking for the usual dealer types. Not that they really have a type in Paradise Factory. It's not like the Haçienda, where they'd still be queuing round the block to get in and then once you do it's so packed it really is each man for himself, especially when it comes to the pursuit of finding party favours.

'Thank you, St Anthony, for finding us drugs,' I say under my breath, while doing a multispeed 'name of the Father' sign of the cross in case any of the other punters see me, which fills me with guilt and remorse, but needs must, as my namesake patron saint is not a reluctant one, just like God – he either loves me with all my faults or doesn't at all. I quickly edit my request:

'Thank you, St Anthony, for finding us drugs that won't kill us.' That feels more sincere, like I'm watching out for us. I'm sure to be shown mercy now with this more appropriate submission of prayer – we only want to partake if it's done safely for all those involved. We can't be dying at Aunty Doreen's house – the poor woman doesn't even know us. What an awful thing to come home to and what a burden on poor Andrew.

'Look out for anyone with wild eyes or chewing,' I tell Matt. You can usually spot someone 'on it' but so far everyone looks quite normal, apart from the nun on roller skates who is also the DJ on the pop floor. But he works here, so it's probably not the best idea.

'OK,' says Matt, me knowing full well that even if he does spot someone that may be able to assist us in our quest for some 'little fellas', as local drug dealer Baz likes to refer to them, he will be too shy to ask and it will be me that does the deed.

More muscled torsos move through into the club, and I spot a guy I've seen at the gym. Dark curly hair and athletic. We've made eye contact a couple of times in the sauna but I always look away in fear. *I wish I could talk to him.* Of course, out of all the times to see him outside the gym it's in this place, but with Andrew's house party beckoning there's no chance.

'Anthony! There's Kenny,' shouts Matt in my ear. I look over to where he's discreetly pointing and he's right. *Thank God. Or St Anthony. Always delivers right on time.*

Kenny is our mutual friend. Works at the BBC.

Lovely, sweet guy who also loves a party. I've ended up back at his a few times after what starts as a 'few drinks and possibly dinner' turns into me picking up the bill for whatever his dealer can deliver. Kenny is no hanger on, though, he's a sensitive type and also has a piano. God knows he's had to put up with my coked-up ramblings while insisting he listen to me play all 23 verses of 'Danny Boy' at three in the morning. Or worse still if I'm really feeling confident, 'Wind Beneath My Wings', dedicating it to my dead grandmother and audience of one. Kenny's a classical pianist too, so after I've assaulted his eardrums with my renditions, I then in turn have to sit through his Chopin or Rachmaninoff depending on what level of anxiety the coke is hitting. If anyone knows how to score in this place, though, it's Kenny, so after a quick double vodka and Red Bull each we saunter over.

'Oh, my God! Fancy seeing you here.'

'Oh, hi Kav, hi Matt!' Kenny is pleased to see us as are we him, even if it is mainly to ask him where to get some stuff.

Small talk ensues over the music, and I wait for a moment to drop a hint. With the vodka and Red Bull and three Red Stripes before that now doing what it's supposed to I figure there's no time like the present.

'I don't suppose you know anyone that can, or if you happen to have any, er . . .'

'Pills?' Kenny replies.

Hallelujah

'Yes! It's just that we're going to a boring house party

and need a couple to get us through the night, if you know what I mean?!'

'No, sorry, I don't have any, Kav. It's a bit early but there will be some flying around later I'm sure.'

Fuck. Not only have I made it appear that I'm not even hanging around to spend time with him, it now looks like I'm only saying hello to ask for drugs.

'I *do* have these, though,' he declares, reaching into his pocket with a smile.

Kenny, disco Willy Wonka to my drug-greedy Augustus Gloop, then opens the palm of his hand under his denim jacket while beckoning me to take a peek, revealing three tiny paper or possibly cardboard dots staring back at me.

'Oh!' I say, trying not to sound disappointed that whatever these things are they are not a pill of any kind so therefore won't touch the sides.

'Yes, we brought them back from Glastonbury and don't need them, if you want to buy them off me?'

Need? What does he mean, 'Don't need them'? Why? What do they do? Surely not that much judging by the size of them.

'OK, I'll buy them off you,' I say, realising beggars can't be choosers, and we have the indie party from hell to attend and we can't be late for Andrew.

'Just be careful,' warns Kenny. 'They are very strong, just bite a bit off of one each.'

'OK. Thanks *so* much, Kenny. I'll be back home again in a couple of weeks, let's do dinner.'

The sweet relief of at least scoring something washes

over me while Matt goes for his fourth piss of the night, and I go outside to hail a cab for us to get to the party.

Once inside the cab, Matt pulls out the remaining dregs of Red Stripe he's smuggled under his jacket, and I inspect the three dots of paper I've just purchased.

'They look like trips,' says Matt, suddenly the connoisseur of all things narcotic.

'What's a trip?' I reply, feeling a bit silly that me, the now so-called well-travelled pop star and man of the world, knows less than my mate Matt, the postman who I assumed had only been introduced to anything remotely narcotic through me.

'Clive has 'em at work. He loves 'em. He says they mash you right up.'

I'm not sure the word 'mash' it what I was looking for, but in for a penny . . .

'Shall we just take a bit each, then?'

With that I bite into the tiny bit of paper and pass the other bit to Matt, both swigging it down with the now near-flat Red Stripe.

'Fuck it. What's the worst that can happen anyway?'

I stare out the window watching the northern city lights. I'm away so much now, living out of a suitcase here, there and everywhere for months at a time. It feels good to be home. Even the short breaks, I'm glad I get to spend them with the likes of Matt and Andrew, the friends that really know me and that aren't impressed by any of the pop stuff or how rich I now am.

'No drinking in the car, lads,' says Mr Taxi Driver.

'Sorry, it's just your next left then right to the end and we'll get out by the off-licence, please.'

I pay up and we head into the off-licence for supplies. Mark randomly stares at the dog food while I go in search for some mixers. I notice the fridge light flicker off and on, and for some reason it's making a sound like a humming, vibrating engine, which suddenly becomes deafening in my ears. *They can't STILL be ringing from the nightclub?* I walk over to the till and look at the top shelf in search of the vodka. I notice a blue elephant of the Indian idol Ganesh sitting on top of the mini CCTV camera above.

It winks at me.

The next two to 26 hours are, shall we say, a bit of a blur and I'm not just referring to the *Parklife* album that seemed to be on repeat for the first part of our night either. Upon arriving at the terraced house where Andrew was throwing the party, not only did Matt – who had by now turned as white as a ghost – and I realise we were in for a bumpy night and that these little dots of paper may have granted us a one-way ticket to Pluto, but I realised that I was stood on the very same street where the Scout hut had been when I was in the Cubs at age 10. The very same Scout hut where our Scout Master hanged himself years later, God rest his soul. This then set a macabre tone in my mind while also wondering why Aunty Doreen's doorbell was in fact an elephant's tusk and why her swinging begonia plant in the hanging basket overheard was wrapped in a grey and hair-ridden trunk.

'Just breathe, we can't let them see we're completely off it,' I whisper to Matt.

'I'm scared, Anthony, and I can't feel my fingers,' cries Matt, whose face seems to have suddenly shape-shifted into a smiling lizard with a red baby bow on his head. *Jesus.*

Once indoors, and after we've sheepishly said our hellos to Andrew and some of his new student pals, we grab a bottle of weak beer and leave our carrier bags of just-bought booze on the kitchen counter. *Last thing we need is strong spirits, we need to let this stuff wear off.* That is until the pair of us decide it's not doing its proper job as we only took a teeny bit and of course to get the full more pleasurable experience of the trip we should take a full one, which we then do and, like a drug-fucked Laurel and Hardy, retreat to the corner of the living room, sitting cross-legged opposite each other looking absolutely suspicious. It's at this perfectly well-timed moment Andrew's sister Eliza appears from the kitchen. I remember Andrew's little sister growing up and she was a cute little thing with a cheeky smile who always had you laughing. Not anymore, it seems like. Eliza, who I haven't seen in years, is now a confident woman of the world and has suspicions of our foul play.

'Av yous two 'ad trips?' she asks, arms crossed and eyes full of disgust.

The sweet little Eliza I remember is now long gone and has been replaced with Moston's own Miss Trunchbull but with a Manc accent. How on earth she knows this is a mystery. Could be the rocking back and forth perhaps . . .

Matt and I stare at each other, waiting for the other to say something, but are too preoccupied keeping the canoe that we are now in, riding Aunty Doreen's swirling carpet of beetles and sea snakes, to reply. I know Matt's seeing the same horrors as me as we both ducked at exactly the same time the African green parrot just flew past.

'Er, no,' is all I can reply.

We make our excuses and leave. Excuses being, 'WE.HAVE.TO.GO,' then bolt out the door into the now pissing-down rain. A walk, we decide, regardless of the weather, is what's needed to let this thing pass through us. Little do we realise it will be another 12 hours of hell involving being convinced that we are being followed by a giant Alsatian dog, an altercation with a breathing lamppost and ending up at back at my mum and dad's in the dead of night where we become certain my mother's Pierrot clown ornament on the living-room mantelpiece is in fact an all-singing-and-dancing demonic Lisa Stansfield.

* * *

Wake-up calls at 4am are no joke, especially when you're still coming down from an almighty first (and most definitely last) acid trip. You'd have thought that me knowing I had a TV appearance on *The Big Breakfast* would have curbed my gallivanting at the weekend, but, oh no, not me. Poor Matt is back on his postman shift this morning too, so God knows how he feels. The last I saw of Matt was him walking like a robot into a taxi at dawn from my mum and dad's while they were sleeping, oblivious to the fact their beloved son and his best mate were busy talking to ornaments and going through LSD psychosis in their living room. Having hardly slept and feeling like I've just survived a lobotomy, I still feel the remnants of 'the trip', and the slightest sound in my ears or imagined shadow on the wall gives me the heebie-jeebies. Of course, I have to put on a show for my live interview, but this morning feels like particularly hard work.

'It's a fun segment with Zig and Zag, they are pretty crazy!' Zig and Zag, who the bubbly runner has just mentioned, are the show's Irish furry puppets, known for their chaotic and cheeky presenting and piss-taking of their celebrity guests. This was not in the memo. I was hoping it would be me and one of the human presenters at least. Not that I bothered looking at any itinerary in the first place. It took copious amounts of Berocca, three snooze buttons on my phone and a vat of coffee just to get me out the hotel room this morning, if you can even call getting up at 4am 'morning'. I smile back and just say 'Great' while knowing full well it wasn't that long ago that I was seeing demons and staring at a brass doorknob for eight hours riddled with panic.

I have my own make-up artist now, called Ally, who is running unusually late. I shudder every time I have to ask where she is when the runner pops her head in the door to check on the time.

I always feel like some precocious little Lord Fauntleroy when having to explain to people I have a travelling person that attends to my 'grooming'. I mean, come on, it's only a bit of powder to stop the sweating under the lights of whichever job you're on and a bit of styling for the hair. Still, Virgin pay lovely Ally for the privilege so it all adds up. Finally she arrives and my heart starts beating inside my chest again.

Needless to say, my seven-minute appearance with the puppets is terrifying. I have my cap pulled down as far as I can as I still feel my eyes are twitching. I was definitely not at my best. Skin of my teeth, I'd say. I head back to the Maida Vale hotel where Virgin now put their pop acts like me, 911 and Billie, wondering what in the name of David Lynch just happened, and crawl into my bed. It's still only 11:30am. I manage to drift off to sleep while the world carries on outside – the sounds of London buses and the calls of the greengrocers on Kilburn High Road. I pray I get some sleep. I do. Finally.

ALL GROWN UP

Moston, 1997

Mother is convinced the next-door neighbour is a prostitute. A 'lady of the night' as she puts it. Although she and Father are grateful I bought them a house, there always seems to be a new issue with it. Moving two people in their late sixties was never going to be a walk in the park, but if it isn't the noise of the railway track close by or the fact that they can see other neighbours walking past the newly fitted patio windows it's something else. It's not my fault we lived behind a jungle of overgrown privet bushes in the last place, thanks to the council never getting it done. It is my duty to be somewhat the adult, though, as they didn't ask to move. Nor do they understand the logistics of what it entails, having never owned a house themselves or even had a mortgage. I am now co-parenting my parents while also trying to navigate this new pop-star life. They weren't keen on moving out of Moston when we started looking for this new place, so we eventually settled on a cosy little Brookside Close-style house. It looked like a show home, which seemed to make Mother and Father overlook that the shared driveway and next door's front door were more or less next to ours.

'She's always banging that bloody door,' Mum says, on the phone to me while I'm on a break from rehearsing for the *Smash Hits* Poll Winners Party and attempting to tell her that it's going to be on the telly on Sunday on BBC One at 5pm.

'I'm going to be winning an award, Mother. *An award.*'

'Not just in the day either. She was banging it at two o'clock in the morning as well. A man in a car came to pick her up. It won't be the first time either!'

The thing is, as much as we LOVE our Rita and there is no doubt she is the best mother any child could have asked for, she has over the years had a tendency to, shall we say, lie about the odd thing. Actually, I take it back – how about a tendency to embellish to, you know, make things seem a bit more interesting, entertaining like.

'Is Dad there? You need to write it down in case you forget what time, which I know you won't but . . .'

'And another thing – she's been wearing high heels and a short skirt! At two o'clock in the pissin' mornin'?! I can't be living next to a woman scorned!'

I won't bother correcting her that it's more likely my mother who feels scorned not Christine the next-door neighbour, who on the odd occasion I've seen her was

carrying a green Marks & Spencer bag with a copy of
Hello! magazine – not even *OK!* And not a high heel
in sight. I'd say more a sensible court shoe, actually.
Hardly a woman that looks like she's moonlighting
as a 24/7 escort.

'I'll sort it out when I get back, don't worry, Mum. Is
Mickey there?' I ask, in order to change the subject, but
sounding like I've actually asked her to pass the phone
to the cat.

'Course he bleedin' is. Your father's fed him this
morning and he's laddered my tights twice this week.'

'Aaahh, good. OK, well I'll call on Sunday to remind
you and Dad about the awards thing.'

'Oh yes, call on Sunday then, yes. When will you be
coming home?'

I don't like this question. I'm currently on a German
radio tour and I miss them, and it makes me feel guilty
that I'm not there. I've taken them out of their familiar
world and dumped them in a show home on the
outskirts of what they know and just left them. Sure,
it looks good on paper, and it sounds good coming out
of my mouth: 'I bought my parents a house.' Martyring
myself at the altar of the precious, caring son. But at
what cost? The place is only a quarter the size of the
council house and let's face it, that was more or less
paid for them anyway, so me buying this place outright
and proudly saying there's no mortgage makes no odds
to them, does it? A selfish move. I am lonely. And I
am selfish. This is not working. This is not what I'm
supposed to be feeling.

I must not be ungrateful. I am so lucky. Remember what you wished for.

'I'll be home soon, Mum, I promise. But remember, I'll call on Sunday!'

'OK, son. Ta-ra, then.'

'Ta-ra, Mum.'

MTV HANGING OUT

Today I will perform live with a band for the first time ever. OK, I will have a band behind me who will mime to the track, but it makes a change from me being on my own. I will sing live, though, on an MTV show called *Hanging Out* where I will be the 'musical guest' and also be interviewed by the super-cool host Davina McCall, who I've watched a few times and seems lovely.

The first bit we film is where Davina will pretend to be spying on my dressing room, and I open the door and catch her. It goes well and she makes me feel at ease straight away. I arrived this morning from Manchester, after a quick visit to see Mum and Dad, and ended up partying a bit late with some northern celebrity pals till the early hours on Sunday. I only realised when I arrived into my dressing room that the Helmut Lang rubbery grey jacket I'll be wearing for my performance had a wrap of coke left inside the pocket. At this point,

I've only done this stuff a few times, but when I have done it I seem to want to do more and more. Now I know I've got some I'm wondering if I should have some before the interview to give me a perk or some confidence. From what I've seen lately, everyone's at it, not just us 'celebs' but even the record company people during the day at work! When I was at Virgin HQ last week a bike delivered some 'records' and guess what was hidden inside? Yup! Thing is, I've only ever done the stuff after feeling a bit drunk, so it could be a risk doing it stone-cold sober. *What's the worst that could happen, though, really? Davina looks a bit rock-and-roll in her black PVC outfit, but should I offer her any? Is that what you're supposed to do? What exactly are the rules with this stuff? Is it only rock stars that get away with saying they do it? Why not pop stars too? I wonder if any of the boy bands do it?*

Due to the fact it's burning a hole in my pocket and now my mind, I go into the toilet in the dressing room and lock the door. I can hear Ying chatting away to Chris the stylist and Tyler my hairstylist, who's come up from Manchester to fix my hair. I chop out a line on the toilet seat and carefully roll up the 20-pound note I snuck out of my wallet when no one was looking. I flush the chain and do one big sniff. It shoots up my nostril in one go, hitting the back of throat and making me cough.

'You OK in there, Kavvy? We need to make a move soon. Tyler wants to check your hair before we go out on the studio floor.'

I put the wrap of the remainder of the stuff down my sock. I can't risk it falling out of a pocket on live TV, especially since I noticed me and Davina would be sitting on beanbags.

I open the toilet door and face my waiting entourage, suddenly feeling wide awake and very chatty. I slug some water out of a plastic cup by the mirror while secretly checking my nose for any powder or signs of it running, that's all we need on live TV. A proper drink and a cigarette would be the icing on the cake but maybe I can figure that out after. I walk onto the set and see Davina's big smile welcoming me under the suddenly hot studio lights. *Don't fuck this one up.* It's only midday and I'm feeling high as a fucking kite.

'Hello again! You OK?' asks Davina with a sincere smile. I'm praying she's asking if it's because she knows I'm relatively new on the scene and young and that it's a live interview, not because I may look like how I'm starting to feel – paranoid and wired. *Please, God, get me through this.*

'And . . . action!'

I wipe my now sweating hands on my grey nylon matching trousers and do exactly what all good pop stars should do when in doubt, or in my case feel like they are about to have a self-induced panic attack – smile.

SMASH HITS TOUR

November, 1997

I'm talking to Ronan in the hotel bar after the *Smash Hits* tour gig at Newcastle Arena. The vibes are high and I'm glad the Irish lads are on this tour. It's not that easy making friends when you're a solo act, but having been on tour with them before there's a familiarity. More than small talk. There's connection. It doesn't do any harm that I had what I think was some flirting with Stephen on the last tour too, which gives me hope there could be again. Ronan's a genuine guy. I'm feeling all the right feelings. *Great show tonight. Huge crowd. Buzzing.* Two double JD and Cokes and a bit of leftover stuff from last night done in secret and I'm lit. Until he says my nose is bleeding.

'Kav, you're bleeding,' to be polite, while tapping his right upper lip under his nose. Adrenaline shoots me up off my seat, scraping the chair legs on the floor and almost knocking over my drink at the Jury's Inn bar, which up until two seconds ago seemed cosy and civilised but has now become a torture chamber of my own making. I pull my cap down like that's going to help somehow and sprint to the men's toilet, using my elbow to barge in while also banging my funny bone. *Ouch*. Bright white tiles. Silver taps and little splats of blood now at my feet and on the previously spotless gleaming-white sink. I'm suddenly in the middle of a Stanley Kubrick film waiting for him to shout 'cut'.

No such luck.

I run to the cubicle, shut the door and start picking at the toilet roll. Of course it's a fresh one. *Why do they make them so fucking hard to find the opening?* More blood drips onto the toilet seat lid. Someone is coming. *Fuck*. No, it's the women's toilet door. *Phew*. Deep breaths. Can't find the opening of the toilet paper. More blood. The taste of metal and cocaine and possibly baby powder drips down my throat. I keep tugging at the toilet paper and manage to rip a whole chunk off which I slam to my face and leaking nostril. I try to get more but it's now splitting in half it's so thin, like tracing paper. I place it over the floor tiles, watching it instantly soak the blood, turning it red. An unwelcome past memory of my mum's sanitary towels that I'd see in the bin as a kid flash in my mind. Helen Harper they were called. A woman with brown hair smiling on the front.

I've overdone it again. I simply don't know when to stop lately. When others decide they've had enough and want to call it a night I go back to my room and feel the need to carry on. (When I say 'others' I'm not talking about the lads from Boyzone. The most I've seen those boys get up to is a few late-night drinks in the bar.) I saw a documentary on lab mice being fed the stuff once and they kept going back for more. Little scurrying mice, all jittery and riddled with nerves. Tiny claws scratching against the ground. That's me. A greedy cocaine mouse.

I splash my face with cold water and wipe any remnants of blood away from my nose and upper lip. The gush has at least stopped for now. I wet a bit of toilet paper, roll it into a ball and put it up the nostril that was bleeding to block any more coming out just in case, stuffing it just far up enough to stop the drip and leave it lodged in there. I'll have to make do with breathing out of one nostril for now. Charming.

Back in the warm Jury's Inn bar the lighting seems dimmer, thank God, or it could just be my eyes adjusting from the bright white bathroom. Someone from the tour crew has taken my seat opposite Ronan, which makes sense considering I've probably been in the toilet dealing with the bloodbath longer than I thought, so I huddle in next to one of my backing dancers, Lisa, who's also arrived post-show and is drinking a pint of lager, her drink of choice being a self-confessed ladette and proud of it.

'You OK, Kav?' asks Ronan across the table.

'Oh yeah, fine. I must have bit my lip,' I reply, which makes no sense to either of us.

'Aaah, right,' he says. He looks disappointed, concerned, sorry for me almost. He's either totally oblivious or appalled that I'm lying through my teeth, or more to the point my tissue-bunged nostril.

I notice that Ronan has some stubble and it suits him, brings out his almost perfect jawline, makes him more chiselled, handsome like an actor rather than a boy-band singer. I wonder if he's secretly . . . *Fuck's sake, don't be stupid. He's got a girlfriend. Really cool girl. They joined me and my family for dinner in Dublin. Dead normal, down to earth. Duck and chips she ordered. Love that. Normality. That's what I need. A partner that I can have dinner with, not getting up to no good in hotel toilets alone.*

'SHOTS, SHOTS, SHOTS!'

Dancer Lisa, oblivious to my secret internal paranoia, breaks the ice by demanding a round of tequilas for the table, a welcome interruption amid me trying to figure out how to get myself out of this mess. *Do I add insult to injury by embellishing my lip-biting accident with Ronan or just carry on as if nothing's happened?* I go for the latter option. *This is not good.* I fucking hate myself for doing this and possibly exposing myself in this way. Just as I'm starting to get to know Stephen, too. I'm aware of how close Stephen, or 'Steo' as they clearly lovingly call him, is with the other boys in the group. I see them looking over when him and I chat sometimes and wonder if he's told them he likes me. *Do they know?* I want them to think I'm a good person for Stephen, not some stupid party boy who gets drunk and does drugs. *Why did I not just stick to having a few drinks tonight instead of doing the other stuff? Fuck*. Hopefully Ronan will give me the benefit of the doubt and go along with my not-so-convincing lip-biting story.

The hotel bar starts to fill up more. I'm too on edge to chat, though, so I do the only thing that I know will give me a chance of relaxing – drink more.

Two double JD and Cokes will do that. The edginess from the cocaine has worn off and I daren't do any more. Although I could do with removing the ball of tissue at some point, but no one's batted an eyelid and I'm too busy mingling and coming down from the show. Stephen's been here a while now and our eyes have met more than a couple of times, waiting for either one of us to look away first. It was me the first time. I'm not used to this and I've also been busy chatting to the road crew and the odd fan who has found their way in. I could learn a lot from Stephen. I often get too friendly with the fans, forgetting that fan is short for 'fanatic', and although most are really sweet and I see them as friends almost, you do get the odd one that never seems to be satisfied with a little chat or a pic and can throw daggers or even shout abuse if you don't give them enough time. Stephen, on the other hand, is calm and seems to enjoy spending time with them. Maybe they show him more respect because Boyzone have five members and are a huge arena-sellout group, compared to my solo 'star in the making' and overcompensation of being a bit cheeky to hide my true self. Stephen *is* just himself so maybe they respect that and see through my façade?

He eventually walks over to greet me and extends out a big hug.

'What's the story, Anto?' he asks in his gentle Dublin accent mid-embrace, smelling perfect. He's been calling me that ever since I told him my first name was Anthony and I love that he does it. Another new name for me, but unlike 'Kav' this one feels like home, albeit with an Irish twist.

'How's Steo?' I say nervously, hoping I've not blown it by seeming too overfamiliar using the name his best friends in the band call him, but at the same time feeling the first genuine smile I've been able to make all night.

'All the better for seeing you,' he says, as if I was the best surprise of his day, immediately making me forget the internal panic I've been going through so far tonight. I think I blush, but it's fine.

That smile.

We talk about the show and he compliments me on my set. I do the same with him. It's a bit small-talky but it's OK. The language isn't what matters, really. It's the feelings that happen every time he's near me. They are a whole lot diffcrent to the feelings I've felt with the only other man I've been close to. There's no power dynamic, no desperate need for approval, no emotional booby traps. I'm just myself and it feels like he is too. God knows how I'd ever get to kiss him. I want to kiss him.

We carry on our chat back at the table where some of the other guys from the band, including Ronan and a couple of their dancers, are now sitting. I've still got the ball of tissue shoved up my nostril but I have some-how forgotten about what happened pre-Steo arriving and am feeling calm and relaxed. What seems like 10 minutes has been an hour and it's getting late as, one by one, the bar starts to empty along with our table, leaving just myself, Ronan and Stephen.

'I think I'll call it a night, lads,' says Ronan, with a genuine yawn. I'm not tired and it's nothing to do with the drugs that have by now thankfully worn off and been replaced with the tranquilising effects of the alcohol and Stephen's presence. I'd normally be shy and nervous around someone I fancied but it wasn't like that with him.

'It's late. I'll probably go to bed too,' says Stephen, making me wonder if our deep connection is all in my head. I say nothing but grab my jacket and phone and leave the bar with the others.

All three of us get in the lift. Ronan's room is on the same floor as Stephen's and without saying a word I get out with them on their floor, despite my own room being two floors up. I've no idea what I'm doing but my feet keep moving towards wherever Stephen is going while Ronan walks ahead. I don't want the night to end and I've never been so determined for it not to. Stephen keeps talking while we walk towards his room, almost like it's some unspoken agreement we want to be alone together.

'Goodnight, lads,' says Ronan, which feels like his way of saying, 'It's OK with me.'

Hugs all round and it's finally just me and Stephen

standing outside his room. He puts his key card in the door and we go in.

I don't sleep in my hotel-room bed that night, and I get a glimpse of what innocent, real, genuine connection with another feels like.

THE WIN

Earls Court, 30th November, 1997

Ying and I are sitting in my dressing room at the Earls Court Arena, where I am about to perform in front of 30,000 fans at the annual *Smash Hits* Poll Winners Party. As you do. We are sharing a croissant from catering which I'm only picking at, due to feeling fat in the Superman costume I'll be wearing for my performance. I've watched this show religiously for as long as it's been on TV, so to be on it and winning something (that big gold award I've only dreamed of) is surreal and wonderful, but everyone always looks so good, and I feel self-conscious in this bloody get-up I agreed to weeks ago. I should never have said yes to the fitted T-shirt and red trouser combo. For the past month, away on my German radio tour – if it works for NSYNC, it could work for me too, right? – my waist size has gone up two inches thanks to my diet consisting mainly of lard, so minimal food for energy along with press-ups will be in order before showtime.

Rumour has it that Peter Andre and his team (Peter has as many 'team' here today as Janet Jackson, who smiled at me in the corridor?!) may not be happy that I'm winning the Best Male Artist award instead of him and there may also be issues with the running order where he may be on early in the show, unlike me who will be on right after the Spice Girls. Gary Barlow's not complained, and he's come third. With the theme being 'Superheroes', Peter is going to perform as Batman and has an entourage of 16 dancers. I have eight. I've been asked to be Superman, or 'SuperKav', which are the words emblazoned on front of my blue-and-red nylon fitted T-shirt made especially for the show and which is somehow getting tighter each time I try it on.

'Thirty minutes to go, you feeling good? Sorry couldn't help it!' says one of the runners who, judging by her manic smile appears to have upped her Prozac today in order to cope with the biggest party in pop.

'I'm great!' I lie. I'm not great, I'm on edge, as the other worrisome thing on my mind is that it's looking like it may be a no-show from The Manager. I keep going back on the promise I've made myself – to leave him if he doesn't turn up today. I've still not told Ying my plan, which makes me feel guilty as we share (almost) everything. But today is the last straw. This year has been the biggest for me, at least success-wise, and I've only seen him a handful of times, and he mainly communicates through Ying. After everything I've felt for him, is it wrong that I feel pissed off? He surely knows how much this means to me, and quite frankly if he can't be bothered to make an appearance on the biggest day of my career then I was right – he really has lost interest and doesn't see the future I see for myself. Sure, I'm grateful for the amazing opportunity he's given me in the first place, but enough is enough, plus I'm over the lovey-dovey feelings towards him now. I just want respect. I deserve it. I'm scared.

The costume I shall be wearing does in fact look cool but the T-shirt makes me look like a balloon that's due to pop due to feeling bloated from the late-night club sandwich and cheesecake I ordered from room service last night at my fancy lodgings for the weekend – The Chelsea Harbour Hotel, if you please, at the suggestion of my Glaswegian boozy accountant (three words that should never go together) Sandra to 'treat yourself, whack it on the business account, hen!' in celebration of me winning my award. I must be the only fool that has an accountant who tells them to spend money. She is a hoot, though, and I am officially with Coutts bank now, so I may as well enjoy these luxuries once in a while. I do wonder if any other artists go for regular wine-fuelled dinners at the Oxo Tower with their accountants and whack it on their business account at their accountant's suggestion? *Just as well I didn't have the hotel buffet breakfast, as that would have really bloated me up, and I'd have never fitted into the red trousers I'm wearing as part of the get-up.*

THE WIN

My performance for the show has been choreographed by Phil Griffin who's directed a couple of my videos and knows my limits when it comes to dancing, so although I shall be busting some moves, it's my troupe of dancers, each one in matching red-and-black outfits and faces covered in lace masks to add a touch of superhero mystery, that will be doing the real work. I, however, have the task of transforming from Clark Kent to Superman/Kav live on air mid-performance and, so far in rehearsals, I can't get the long black coat and glasses off in time for the first bar of the chorus of my song for the big reveal, as said coat weighs a ton. It *has* to be slick, and it *has* to work.

Outside the dressing room, I hear the anxiety-inducing sound of a football bouncing and laddish voices. Doesn't matter where I am, it still takes me right back to the feeling of dread – either dread I'm about to not be picked again for the school football team, or dread one of the lads round ours that's bouncing their ball on our wall is about to shout 'poof' or 'gay boy' as I white-knuckle it to the newsagents to get my magazines. The racket comes from a new boy band called Five or '5ive', if we keep to their branding. They will be winning Best New Group today, and they seem nice enough, apart from one who always seems to give me daggers. Maybe it's me and my laddie paranoia, but I swear every time we catch each other's eyeline it's like he wants to punch me. Maybe he thinks I'm rude for not speaking to him, but I'm not, I'm just shy with most other male pop stars. Scared they will see the real me which is someone

I'm not sure I even see these days. Maybe he mistakes my shyness for being aloof, or maybe he mistakes me laughing and joking with my female backing dancers as flirting with them, or that I'm having sex with them. Little does he realise I'm barely getting it on with myself let alone another human.

There's another knock at the door – it's Mel C and Geri from the Spice Girls. They are winning Best Group of course and are practically royalty these days – we've come a long way since we were the surprise acts for the Virgin Records summer ball, drunk on Hooch and dreaming of pop stardom. They've since been a worldwide smash, but here they are knocking on *my* door? Geri sits herself down in the make-up chair next to mine and looks as though she's about to tell me something important. A real heart-to-heart it seems. *Gulp.* I've never actually spoken to Geri one-on-one before, I'm more pals with the two Mels and Emma (Posh remains quiet to me), so the fact that she takes my hand in hers is a shock and makes me wonder what in the name of new best friends is happening.

'You are *so* talented,' she says, big blue eyes like saucers staring deep into mine. There's so much intensity in how she's talking I'm half expecting her to whip out a crystal ball next. 'I'm really, truly proud of you.'

Blimey. Proud of me? What have I done to warrant such seemingly sincere praise from one fifth of the biggest pop group in the world currently?

'This is huge for you today – Best Male Artist – you could be the next George Michael, you know.'

I know some pop stars aren't known for their subtleties, but this is on another scale. Yet she seems so intensely loving and sincere that I have to believe she means it. Either that or she's dropped an E.

'Wow, er . . . Thank you, Geri. That means a lot,' I reply, sincerely meaning it in return. I think of something else to say, but before I can find the words, she's out the door, gone, leaving me in a warm fuzzy daze.

Have I just had my career blessed at the altar of Ginger Spice? Maybe. Either way, I now feel on top of the world. I polish the lenses of my Clark Kent glasses and put on the coat, which suddenly feels much lighter. I smile to myself while running my dad's lucky comb through my Brylcreemed slicked-back hair one last time. I really am doing good after all. Everything is working out as it should. I better enjoy this joyous connection to the universe while I can, however, as in a few hours' time I'll be back in my Chelsea Harbour suite, celebrating my huge win alone, downing vodka and champagne while snorting lines of coke off my shiny new *Smash Hits* award made of tin.

ONE WEEK LATER

I am leaving The Manager. To be honest, I already have mentally. When presenter Jayne Middlemiss – dressed as Catwoman – handed me my *Smash Hits* award live on air I made sure I said 'I want to thank my manager' and that was it. There and then, that was the moment, except only I knew it. The man who made all my dreams come true and showed me love and attention. The person who awakened a spark in me that now refuses to go out, an all-day-and-night secret longing for connection with another man. The brief yet special one I had with Stephen was impossible to continue. Both of us with non-stop itineraries and constantly being at airports or hotels or wherever. I longed to see the Irish +353 code come up in my phone and I looked forward to our late-night chats, but I have no idea what boundaries are in relationships and go from feeling obsessed to disillusioned in the space of a text or lack of reply. My decision to leave The Manager has not been an easy one and actually feels more like what a break-up with a boyfriend would be like, that's if I ever have one now. It's pretty clear he seems to have lost interest. I have no idea what he's doing behind the scenes but as far as being the caring man I first met, those days are long gone. I need someone who sees the bigger picture. He has no idea of the potential of where my career can go. How could he if we hardly talk? I have no issues with what went on between us. I'm 19 years old now. Not a kid. I played a part in it too but he acts like the special bond we have is gone. It's not fair. Or if he feels bad then there's even more reason to check in with me and ask me how I am and tell me how proud he is of me. I've just won a *Smash Hits* award for God's sake! The one he promised to show up for and didn't. Yeah, that one.

I'm too nervous to tell him over the phone so I hand-write the letter explaining from the heart (leaving out anything *too* personal in case someone else in the office sees it) how grateful I am for what he's done for me. I explain it's time to move on now. I of course have no idea what I'm doing, but I can't carry on feeling not just professionally but emotionally let down by him. Maybe one day I'll see why he's acting like he's not interested, but for now I know I have to cut ties.

Being a little more worldly and ambitious, and also being saved career-wise by winning Best Male at the *Smash Hits* awards right in the nick of time, I end up signing with Pete Evans at Native, who also happens to be Simon Fuller's right hand man at 19 Management which Native is under the umbrella of. New blood.

A fresh start. Pete takes over managerial duties and puts all his efforts into cleaning up the mess I didn't realise I was in with Virgin and the old boss. I was right, if it wasn't for me winning the award which proved I beat a handful of the UK's other front runners of male singers I may also have been dropped. Great. Talk about skin of my teeth.

Meanwhile my sincere and from-the-heart letter to The Manager doesn't go down too well. I receive a typed letter back in the post a day or so after I've sent mine. Think of a balloon made of 10 tons of lead laced with vitriol and resentment and you'd be half on the money. There is no accountability, no sense of even attempting to understand my point of view. Just, in a nutshell, that I'm wrong and I've made a mistake and I will regret it, especially after everything he's done for me. I'm not sure what I was expecting in reply from the man who after all did change my life and give me this chance, but I wonder if he's right and if I have made a mistake? *Have I got carried away? Do I owe everything to him, and if I do for how long? Forever?* I sense an element of threat in his words. Only he knows my secret. Only he knows who I really am. I feel terrified I've fucked everything up. *Will he out me?* Even if not publicly, he could tell people in the industry that the boy he took from a council house and turned into a pop star with a huge record deal and even lent thousands to buy a house for his parents has betrayed him and is also actually gay. It's not the best look now I'm at the peak of my career, almost looking like I've got too big for my boots and forgetting who made me who I am in the first place. *Fuck*. Meanwhile all I can say in my pathetic explanation of why I've left him is because I feel he 'lost interest in me'. How childish and spoiled it sounds now.

I suppose this outcome was to be expected, really. He's not exactly going to be jumping for joy. I should have known something was up from the frantic missed calls I got from his office number as soon as they probably received my letter.

The next day I flee to Mum and Dad's house, but I feel too nervous being in the same city as The Manager or any of my now old management company workers who I could bump into if I head into the city centre, which is the only other place I go when I'm home. I have a week off from promo so get a night flight to London – a costly last-minute decision but my anxiety couldn't even cope with a two-hour train ride – and check in to a random hotel and hide for a week until it all dies down. I suddenly feel grown up and professional. *Thank God for having money and independence to just up and disappear for a bit*. The first taste of having too much time on my hands, however, coupled with my over-sensitive mind doesn't fare well with my self-imposed isolation and around-the-clock topped-up minibar, feeding my now more regular drinking habit. I wander late at night round Soho and dare myself to go into some of the gay bars alone but I don't. I just walk and walk instead. Worrying if I've made the right decision and nervous of what the consequences could be if I've not.

LUCKY BOY

'It's looking like it could be Germany or Italy,' says my new manager Pete over the phone, who since coming on board not only sorted out the next album contract with a hefty advance to boot but is also getting his now huge producer clients Absolute – who produced my first top 10, 'I Can Make You Feel Good' – to co-write and produce the whole record. With their last two records being the Spice Girls albums these guys are pop's hot property right now. We also get on like a house on fire so I can be totally (almost) myself around them. Pete also mentions that it looks like Mark 'Spike' Stent – who is one of the biggest mixers out there, having done Madonna's last record – will be available to mix it too. God knows how he's convinced them, although I am now officially a Best Male Singer according to *Smash Hits* so I'll take it all while I can. The only issue is where we'll record it. I hadn't had the most delightful of times so far on my trips to Germany, mainly because it rained, no one really knew who I was, and I spent most of the time hungover after being introduced to Jägermeister by the eighties rocker-looking record company A&R guy who I spent most of the evenings in the hotel bar with discussing such topics as the political importance of The Scorpions 'Winds of Change' and how Germany's biggest selling group The Kelly Family may possibly be inbred.

Italy, though, well now we're talking! What's not to love? The culture, the food, the wine, the sunshine. Not to mention the beauty of the people. And last year I had my very own TV special there on cult show *Roxy Bar* with Red Ronnie who is Italy's Jools Holland meets Terry Wogan where I performed songs and took questions from the Italian fans. *Surely it makes more sense to go there. Per favore, God. Maybe Mother could risk her lifetime fear of flying and I could take her to the Vatican while I'm at it.*

In the meantime, while the plans for my second album are afoot, I have some time off, as in a whole six weeks to be exact. I don't feel like staying in hotels in London, and although I could go to Manchester to be with Mum and Dad or even go to Cornwall to see my sister and brother-in-law, I feel like a big change is needed before I dive into my next big creative season. I feel like I need a reboot. There is also talk of a big summer tour of Southeast Asia, Australia and New Zealand after the album's finished recording, so these next couple of months are really the only time I will have to focus on me for a change.

I'm also aware there have been rumblings about my weight. Nothing offensive and not something to worry about too much but it's been gently suggested more than once to 'get in the gym,' said more like, 'Oh yes, you can really use this time to work on song ideas, you know, get back in the gym, maybe?' It's the 'maybe' that doesn't sit right. Are you (a) suggesting I have time off to do what I want and exercising being one of them (it's not), or (b) implying I may have piled on a few pounds since living in hotels of late and comfort eating and drinking to take the edge off all the big changes I've brought on myself for the most part (I have)? After a good more-liquid-than-lunch meeting with my accountant, and because she knows my money better than me, we decide over the second course at Pitcher & Piano Trafalgar Square (nearest to her office – signing off huge cheques is much more fun when you're a bit squiffy) that not only will I get a fitness trainer to show everyone I mean business with what's sure to be my huge comeback record *but* I will be going to LOS ANGELES to work with the best one there is! Three bottles of Pinot Noir have a lot to answer for it seems, especially when orchestrating a master plan for your career.

Sandra says she has friends in high places, mainly her clients, one of them being another huge pop manager who she does the accounts for, and with a few phone calls she was able to find me someone. It was me that suggested LA, as I've been wanting to go on a music-writing trip out there for some time, and even though

I'll be writing most of the new album with my new producers, it can only add to my creativity to write with some of the big US guns and also extend my trip to work with this mysterious fitness trainer. I should have gone for the sticky toffee pudding after all, as I may as well enjoy the calories while I can. Wheatgrass shots and egg whites here I come, not to mention no one will recognise me out there so I could go to the gay bars without a care in the world. Who said money can't buy you happiness, eh?

I pay the bill without even looking at it while Sandra yaps away on her mobile seemingly about me and what we just discussed. *Eek*. We head back to her office. Apparently a fax is being sent for us to look at with some quotes from this personal trainer to the stars called Greg. Sandra does not mess about. This guy trained Demi Moore for *G.I. Jane* and has just finished working on set with Tobey Maguire for *Spider-Man* apparently. Blimey.

We look at each other and giggle. I just love her positivity and 'yes you can' attitude.

'You really are amazing. Thank you for sorting this out for me, Sand!' I say. 'I was just wondering how much it might cost?'

'I'm sure I heard about two grand a week over the phone but it was so noisy in there; it will be on the fax, plus we will need to add your hotel and flights and living money out there. I reckon about £50k at least.'

'Oh, that's not too bad!' I say, wondering if this woman has lost her mind or am I just in fact naive to having money and that it is there to be spent after all? 'And you're sure we can afford it?'

'Och, aye!' Sandra reassures me, almost offended at my question and now extra Scottish to show how ridiculous my concerns are over my own finances. 'This is no time to be worrying about money! This is an investment. You're going to be a superstar, hen! We will have to look at getting you a place to stay too – only the best for my pop star,' she says, slugging down the last bit of wine.

'Oh, you're going to look stunning,' beams Sandra. 'Plus, never mind Spider-Man, you've already been Superman and now you'll get the muscles to match!'

We stumble out into the now rainy and dark St Martin's Lane. I notice Sandra has bought an extra takeaway bottle of wine and stuffed it in her bag, and we link arms and head inside her office next door, where we can carry on with our masterplan.

'Another bottle won't do us any harm, we can use office mugs!' It feels good to have someone believe in me so much and with no strings attached. If you can't trust your financial adviser out of all people then who the hell can you trust?

THE GLAMOROUS LIFE

Four Seasons Hotel, Beverly Hills, January, 1998

I'm lying horizontal in my new Ralph Lauren grey jogging bottoms and Four Seasons Hotel Beverly Hills white towelling bathrobe, my feet dangling over the side with only one of my free hotel slippers on, the other one peeking out from under the white linen tablecloth-covered trolley where I was served my room service breakfast this morning. My body aches, mainly my shoulders and my inner thighs after using muscles today I never thought existed. It's a good ache, though. An ache that tells me I've achieved something good, which I have. I may also be in love! Well, maybe not *in love* as such, but I've never met anyone or, more to the point, felt such a deep connection with someone almost immediately than I have with Greg, my new personal trainer and all-round amazing human being. No wonder the stars in Hollywood pay him so much money as he is without a doubt worth every single penny – or dollar, rather. I met him the day after I landed when he came over to my hotel to go over our fitness itinerary for the next two months. I was a little nervous as I assumed he would be some macho no-nonsense balls-to-the-wall army-type trainer, but I couldn't have been more mistaken. Greg is everything you expect a Hollywood trainer *not* to be. Sure, he looks nice – a chiselled adonis from the gods – but personality wise he is goofy, mellow, with a self-deprecating sense of humour. He's also very spiritual and practices yoga and has a gentleness to him that I can't really put into words. Greg surfs too and is also no stranger to a little pot here and there. They call marijuana 'pot' out here in sunny California, and he has a little pouch with his 'purest smoothest blend' with a little white pipe. He calls it 'smoking a bowl' and he actually asked if he could have a little after we went over everything.

'Hey, you want to smoke a bowl with me?' he asked.

I told him I better not but would love to another time. When we spoke briefly on the phone the night before we had our first meeting, he suggested I have a think about what I was hoping to achieve physically.

'Get some images of other celebrities whose body shape you admire out of magazines and show me. Dare to dream, dude!'

So, I did. A little too over enthusiastically. I went to the newsstand not far from the hotel and bought a bunch of mags including *Us Weekly*, *Rolling Stone*, *GQ* and *Details*, eagerly tearing out picture after picture of the men I wanted to look like (i.e. secretly fancied) like Matthew McConaughey, Tom Cruise, Leonardo DiCaprio, Ben Affleck. I threw in Ethan Hawke as well to show I had cool taste, and left out the ones whose body shape I figured would make me seem a little too delusional: The Rock and Arnold Schwarzenegger I am not and never will be.

Upon showing my images to Greg he just said, 'Cool! Let's see how we go, but you're going to have to work hard, OK? No cheating. And I need you to do exactly what I tell you to.'

'Yes, master,' I almost said. But instead I just replied to his high five with a 'You got it!' and with that the deal was set.

Tonight, after the workout, I had turkey breast with green beans and brown rice with a side plate of something mushy called polenta, all washed down with a chocolate protein shake, which Greg has organised to be delivered to me by a gourmet catering company used by his clients when requiring the right nutrition on a movie set or in their mansions or wherever. I'm not allowed to eat any food off the hotel menu, which is difficult as it has all my favourites but, if I must, it can only be salad – preferably the 'Cobb' and with no dressing and certainly no croutons.

* * *

The days turn into weeks and before I know it I've been in the City of Angels, and my new favourite place in the world, for one whole month. I've even managed to stick to my at-times-gruelling diet and fitness routine with Greg, who has been whipping me into shape on the daily. Although for the most part I'm exhausted by the time we finish for the day and normally just grab a yellow cab from his gym to the hotel and sit watching TV and nibbling on protein and green vegetables, thanks to my new best friend Greg I have had the chance to see *some* of what Hollywood has to offer. I even at one point accompanied Greg to a private party at well-known Beverly Hills restaurant to the stars, Mr Chow, where I had a couple of vodka sodas (the only alcohol allowed, if at all). I'm finding I don't really miss the booze to be honest anyway, which surprised me at first, having been so dependent on it. Everyone seems to be so into their health and fitness out here, plus who wants a hangover when the sun's beating down on you every day?

I buy a postcard from the gift shop with the Hollywood sign stretched across the front to send to Mum and Dad, telling them of my escapades so far and letting them know their son is having the time of his life and working hard:

Dear Mum and Dad,
Just thought I'd drop you a line to say it's all
going amazing out here! The weather is hot and
sunny, and I've been staying at a hotel where all
the stars stay called The Four Seasons.
My fitness trainer I told you about is called
Greg, and he's looking after me and we get on
SO great! Last night he took me to a party at

a famous restaurant called Mr Chow and I met
Tom Cruise! Anyway, I better go now. Hope
Mickey is OK? Lots of Love. Anthony xxxxx

I didn't really meet Tom Cruise, but if he was there I definitely could have. I miss them and the cat.

I imagine my mother looking at the postcard and parading it round the butchers or the cake shop like she does with the other magazines I'm in. 'Our Anthony's in a film with Tom Cruise in Hollywood,' she will most likely say, adding just a little sprinkle of extra glamour to the tale. The apple doesn't fall far from the tree in the telling-stories department, that's for sure.

On one of my afternoons off, I decide to go for a walk to the local mall. I don't often need to walk anywhere as Greg picks me up or I get taxis, but today I decide to bite the bullet and go exploring by myself. After wandering around the streets with my map in my hand that I can't read, I stumble across a huge store called The Pleasure Chest. It doesn't take me more than a few seconds to realise I'm standing a few metres away from the entrance of A Sex Shop.

XXX VIDEOS. TOYS. GAY. DILDOS. LUBE.

The words flash in front of me. Christ, I've never actually been in a sex shop in my life, let alone one that seems to pride itself on benefitting the type of person that I secretly am. My heart races with excitement. I also immediately remember my hotel TV has a VHS player in it. *Surely I couldn't go in and buy an actual gay porn video and watch it?! How does one even choose?*

Are they just on the wall? I wonder if they have those portable masturbator things? A dildo? Gulp. What will they think of me at the till?

I walk round the block and smoke two Lucky Strike, one straight after the other. I feel focused and strangely wired. Negotiating with myself whether I should or not, knowing full well I will. I walk back round the block one last time and arrive back at the store noticing a muscly guy in jeans and trucker boots proudly carrying out his supply in a black plastic bag that says nothing on the front but may as well just say 'I'm going home to wank'. *I should have brought my rucksack, damn it. What will my sweet handsome bellboy think of me walking back into the orchid-filled marble lobby with that?*

I pull down my recently bought LA Lakers baseball cap, realising that no one knows me anyway, and walk into the place.

'Welcome to the Pleasure Chest!' yells the man behind the counter like his life depends on it.

'Hi,' I smile underneath the peak of my cap, wondering if he needs a megaphone just in case anyone else hasn't spotted my nervous figure walking in.

'How can I help you today?'

'I'm just looking, thanks.'

'Oh, you're from England!!!'

Great.

'Yes, just visiting,' I reply.

'Oh, I love your accent! Anything you need just let me know, OK?'

'OK, thank you,' I murmur weakly, while pretending to browse and finger some little black bracelets that seem to be ridiculously small even for a woman's wrist, let alone a man's.

'Just so you know . . .'

Oh Jesus, he's still going.

'We have more of those cock rings downstairs too.'

Help.

ITALY

May, 1998

I'm sipping a small white wine at 2pm in the self-service British Airways club class lounge, which I am now a fully fledged member of and where I am due to board a one-way flight to Genoa in Italy. I am wearing my go-to Gucci light-wash jeans, a white Calvin Klein fitted T-shirt and my new Versace black soft-leather blazer that I bought on Rodeo Drive last month.

After my what feels like life-affirming (and fat-busting) recent trip to LA, I am now supercharged and feeling fit and ready to make my second album, which was eventually decided will be recorded in a cosy beach-side town called Recco in Genoa on the Ligurian coast. I will live in the villa where the top-of-the-range studio is, along with the studio owner and his family, while my producers, Andrew and Paul aka producers Absolute, will live close by in (no doubt also fancy) rented accommodation with their respective wives and children. I can hardly believe how wonderfully this has all turned out. Not only did Virgin sign me for album number two but EMI Music Publishing have picked up their option too. No wonder they offered me that free glass of champagne at Coutts. After the guilt of leaving The Manager and him more or less telling me it was a huge mistake, it feels like it has all worked out better than I could have imagined. Maybe God does have a plan after all. Speaking of God, I have become obsessed with a book given to me by Greg the trainer as a farewell gift when I was leaving LA after hearing him rave about it. *Conversations with God* is the name and it tells the real-life story of a man who during one of the darkest points in his life decides to write a letter to God asking why such terrible things have happened to him (his house burned to the ground and his wife left him, to be fair) and God only starts bloody answering him through his pen right there in his kitchen! What follows is a whole book where God talks to him and answers his questions. It is now my go-to book every day and has provided me with a new-found faith and understanding of the almighty one who may just be looking out for us after all.

Upon arriving at the airport in Genoa I am met by my personal driver for the whole of my stay here, a delightfully jovial man with white hair, dressed sharply in a black suit and named Mario, who drives me along the coast to my new residence with a cheery smile and not a word of English to be spoken. I, now a little buzzed from the in-flight Italian white wine and Grappa *digestif* (a fire-rocket liquid that could strip paint), take in the perfect Italian coastal view while imagining what my surely fortuitous and inspiring trip may entail. *I wonder what the studio owner, who is apparently named Alberto, will be like? Will he be handsome? Gay or straight? Would we have an affair? What if he's married and in the closet?! Why do all names in Italy seem to end with O?*

What if I just focus on the job at hand instead of daydreaming over-the-top fantasies as per and start thinking about what a brand-new album will sound like instead.

'Is it OK if I have a *cigaretto*?' I ask Mario, in hoping that my faux-Italian accent will make him understand my request.

'*Si, certo, signore!*'

I think that means yes. I rummage around my duty-free carrier bag and rip open the box of Marlboro Lights, pop out the in-car lighter and take a deep inhale, letting the fumes blow out the window and into the breeze. The Mediterranean sun glistens on the sea and the air is warm. A new adventure begins. I honestly could not be happier.

* * *

'George Michael's been busted for exposing himself to a cop in a men's toilet.'

Oh shit. Not George. Not George, one of my musical heroes. The same man who I am yet to meet even though we are on the same label and who apparently told Ray Cooper that he loves my voice.

What started out as a normal day in the studio soon becomes a day of intrigue and discussion as we find out mid-writing session that George has been arrested in Beverly Hills for a 'sexual act' in a public toilet. My first reaction is why on earth would a handsome superstar do such a thing when surely he can have anyone he wants? My second thought is how I really wish we didn't have to talk about anything gay-related, as so far I've managed to skim over anything in that department with the boys. Even if they know my secret or have suspicions, they don't press on it and I want to keep it like that. I decide to play dumb and just keep saying two-syllable comments like, 'Oh wow' and 'No way'. Less said about poor George's situation, the better. I'd be a hypocrite to make fun of the situation as I know only too well what the turmoil of doing things in secret and not wanting anyone to find out feels like. Just as well we have music to create.

'Come on, then, let's get back to it,' I say after what feels like an hour being glued to the Italian news channel where there's footage of helicopters and George in handcuffs. For once I don't have much to add to our usual fun and creative banter, so I start banging out a melody on the piano to invite some distraction. 'It will be lunch soon and this song won't write itself!' I say, hoping they get the hint and that it's more to do with my focused work ethic than my fear of my own sexuality.

The nearly three months on the Italian coast fly by, and it feels like a trip of a lifetime with memories to last forever. I fly my old school pals Mark and Carli out twice for long weekends, and my sister Angela and brother-in-law Clint are also able to visit, where we are driven by Mario to such hotspots as Santa Margherita and Portofino, dining in exclusive restaurants and sipping cocktails while watching the sunset.

My new album sounds a little more grown up, with a much slicker production, and I've found the writing process easy with my new best friends, Andrew and Paul. *Smash Hits* fly out mid-recording to do a shoot for my *fourth* cover for when the first single from the new album comes out in August, and editor Gav and his fun crew shoot me in my element in the studio and in the sea. Inexplicably we are hearing reports that I am now huge in Asia, and it seems Virgin want to get me out there ASAP. While I'm over on that side of the world they want me to drop in some dates in Australia, New Zealand and India too. The new album will be released out there before it even hits the UK, so when my Italian dream comes to an end there is no time off, instead I will fly straight from Italy to Taiwan for a press conference. There are genuine tears as I say goodbye to my new Italian family, including Alberto's grandmother Graziella who waves me into Mario's waiting car.

New memories and what feel like soulful connections make it sad to leave. I think of when Mario collected me at the airport at the start of the trip and how I had no idea of what a special time lay ahead. *Maybe I'll come back and do my next record here too?*

Mario opens the passenger door and helps me with my big green suitcase while I put my cap back on and grab my rucksack. We hug. I will miss my friend.

'*Arrivederci, Antonio!*'

I smile that he remembers my real name, which I told him in passing one day driving to the beach on a day-off tour of the coast.

'Bye, Mario. Thank you for everything. *Ci vediamo presto*!' I reply, hoping he's impressed with my learned phrase which means, 'We'll see each other soon.'

No goodbyes.

'I can't wait it!' he says back, both of us knowing deep down that we probably won't, and that it's just another bittersweet farewell, the end of another season in life, even if this one, for me, has been one of the more special ones.

MADE IN TAIWAN

July, 1998

I fly by myself from Italy to Taiwan, which will be the first stop on my six-week tour of Southeast Asia. I'll be met by my new PA from the new management at the other end who's flying from London. I miss Ying, though. Unfortunately, leaving the old manager also meant having to cut ties with everyone at the company and like a coward I just ran, and didn't even give Ying a proper goodbye, the one who actually *was* there day and night for me. So now, after having to say goodbye to all the Italian crew I've just bonded with for the last three months, it feels like it's pointless getting close to anyone ever again.

After a long sleep I am awoken by the hotel phone to say I need to be in reception to meet the team from Virgin Taiwan who will take me to my first appointment of the day – a record signing at Tower Records, Taipei.

'We haven't had this many people since Jimmy

Lin!' exclaims elegant Roya, the Virgin Taiwan record company woman sitting next to me in the blacked-out minibus as we drive through the streets of the city. I've no idea who this Jimmy Lin is but he must be big as, according to Roya, they've had to cordon off the whole street due to the good few thousand fans who have come to see *me*. This is a shock to say the least. I had an idea I was doing well in Southeast Asia but hearing the words 'closed-off streets' and 'police escorts' (plural) has filled me with panic.

'We have a very busy itinerary so we put this signing in first to create buzz, many TV and radio stations will also be here.'

'Oh yes, that makes sense. I'm still a little jet-lagged but it's all exciting stuff.'

Silence.

I seem to have a knack for filling in the gaps of silence when travelling with new people. I'm not keen on the uncomfortableness it brings, to me at least. I wonder if that's why everyone seems to report back how friendly I am and easy to get on with?

'Did you sleep well, Roya? I loved my hotel bed, it's huge!'

'I don't sleep a lot. I'm too busy,' replies Roya.

'I love your shirt,' I say.

'It's Prada, like the suit we got you.'

I forgot they bought me a grey/green Prada suit yesterday at the mall upon arrival. I will be going to a huge event here with a red carpet, so needs must.

When we arrive at Tower Records, the place is

swarmed, like, the Beatles or Elvis or Madonna swarmed. I've only seen this stuff on TV, this is wild.

'They're all here for me? Is anyone else doing something here today?'

'Yes, Kav! They're all for you!'

'But how? Why?! For me? Oh my God, I just can't believe it!' I hear myself blubbering like a poor man's Sally Field at the Taiwanese Oscars, but before I can cry 'They love me!' Roya gets on a walkie-talkie, which she seems to have had all along perched in her Mulberry dainty bag on her knees in preparation to speak to the team that are now obviously prepped and waiting to deal with us upon arrival. She shouts, 'WE ARE READY!' into the mouthpiece in what, judging by the sea of swarming bodies I can see through the van windows, is about to be a mission impossible of the highest order. *Shit.* With that, at last eight policemen in full uniform surround the door of the car, ready to help me run through the stampede of screaming people into the record store for the signing.

'People are fainting so please be careful,' alerts Roya. *Holy shit. Careful of what, though? Me fainting or careful of somehow stamping over them? My beloved fans?*

'Are you sure we can do this safely? It's not fair on them if they are in danger?' I cry. I do worry, though. It's in my nature to care. You hear all sorts of horror stories about what happens at these types of things and I don't know what I'd do if anything bad happened to anyone. I think I'm on the verge of a panic attack.

But the door opens and I'm bundled out, successfully too, thankfully for both me and everyone else

'Noodles or your salmon?' asks Roya, once inside the record store after getting through the swarms of people by the skin of our teeth, and referring to my lunch order, as we have *a lot* of fans to sign for. She seems to have remembered that I said the salmon, or *sall-mon* as she pronounces it, 'was nice' *once* at dinner, but since then it has become 'your salmon' as in 'your favourite' and she now drops said fish suggestion into every meal order. Either that or she's trying give me mercury poisoning.

We head back to the hotel and I head to my executive suite. I'm still at times in shock at the bizarre life I live, and now this level of success or 'fame' in a foreign country is like nothing even I could have dreamed up. I've also noticed I've not touched a drop from the minibar in the room since I got here. This is good. I'm all too aware I've been burning the candle a bit and it hasn't been doing me any favours if I'm really honest with myself. I must be feeling happy. Let's just hope this success translates back in the UK when the record comes out there soon. It will. It has to.

THE FLOP ERA

November, 1998

Lisa Scott-Lee from pop group Steps is talking to me via our reflection in the dressing-room mirror at the *SMTV* studios, where they and I are due to perform our latest singles on the weekly chart show, *CD:UK*. Theirs is already a top 10 hit called 'Better Best Forgotten', with the title feeling more suited to mine with the midweek chart for 'Will You Wait For Me', my heartfelt ballad and huge radio hit in Asia, an extremely depressing number 29, and with only one day of sales left for that to change it's unlikely to climb much higher. If there really is a School of Pop, it's fair to say my fellow classmates Steps have got all As across the board this term while I've scraped by with two Cs and what feels like a week's detention while being tasked with writing 'I AM A FAILURE' a few hundred times on the blackboard. Chart positions aren't mentioned, thankfully, as we chat about my thoughts on possibly moving to America, which I now realise was an overshare on my part and I should have just kept my dreams of making it stateside to myself. What Lisa doesn't realise is that she is slowly killing me with each word that comes from her perfectly glossed lips.

'What you moving *there* for?'

Anyone would think I've announced I was relocating to Wigan, not Los Angeles.

'I'm big in Asia, you see,' I say, realising this sentence is a cliché and like the joke 'Big in Japan' I've heard said as a piss-take, which makes me feel even more awkward. I've come this far so I of course carry on digging myself into my ever-deeper self-justification hole. 'Most of the other artists in the Asian charts are big American acts too' (making sure I get the 'big' in there), 'so it makes sense for me to try and crack it over there.'

'Not being funny,' Lisa interrupts, 'but you're wasting your time.'

Ouch.

'Look, if you're not that big here at the moment . . .'

She's used 'at the moment'. I can work with this, as it means 'could be again'. *Hope is not lost just yet.*

'. . . then you're not going to make it in America.'

Bang. Straight through the heart. I feel my soul start to leave my body, but there's one last shot, just to make sure I'm fully dead.

'Have you not thought about doing panto?'

I decide to go to the canteen.

Saturday mornings at *CD:UK* are usually chaotic. There's no real pecking order like, say, *Top of the Pops* where cool indie artists tend to stay in their dressing rooms, here we all mix and that helps when you're feeling a bit unpopular. Corridors with pictures of famous ITV presenters from over the years, from Cilla to Des O'Connor all smile back while you anticipate how your performance is about to go. By this point in my career, though, and with my big second album comeback not going exactly to plan, it's fair to say I'm slowly checking out. I sense deep down my time is up as a pop star in the UK, I can feel it my bones and see it on my pop peers' faces. If a look was a pat on the head, then I'd most likely be bald. The magazine covers have stopped, and I've been moved to being 'featured' somewhere in the middle section of whatever ones say yes to having me in that fortnight. Even my faithful *Smash Hits* have had to curb their support by demoting my last feature to the 'The Biscuit Tin' section, which means my run of being a regular cover star has well and truly stopped.

The live performance of my new single 'Will You Wait For Me' goes OK. I sacrificed feeling hot in the black suit jacket I wore as it's a stylish piece by Japanese designer John Rocha, which has a large sewn-on black pearl spider on the back. In my mind it's a bit Bowie-esque, but given the fact that I didn't turn round once to reveal the cool spider to the camera I fear I may have looked like I was attending a funeral, which judging by the dull response from the audience I could well have been – for my own career. They obviously weren't familiar with the song as radio hasn't touched it, and it's only been playlisted on The Box channel, where always optimistic Martin, the TV and radio plugger at Virgin, told me it was 'gaining momentum' even if that means at the speed of a donkey with one leg.

Steps brought the house down as expected, which only added to my insecurity. It doesn't help that they have no ego whatsoever and are possibly the nicest band in pop, which makes my lead balloon of a performance an even more bitter pill to swallow. I've only recently realised that H is actually called Ian, which blows my mind as I'd never have put him down as having a name like that. No issues with Ians at all, but it just doesn't seem very him. It's a bit of an open secret that H is gay too; not only that, but he's dating his manager Tim who also happened to be the producer of the *Smash Hits* Poll Winners Party and told me I'd won Best Male Singer the day before the live show. How so much can change in a couple of years. Where all the thousands of fans have gone, who took the time to tear out the voting form and write my name and then walk to the post office and bloody post it, is a mystery.

I think H knows I'm gay, but he hasn't asked. I had an inkling with him on the *Smash Hits* tour when he would burst into the odd show tune at the soundcheck. *Why would H ask me about being gay, though? If he is in a relationship with his manager, he's not going to be asking me my business.* I sometimes wish people wore badges saying what sexuality they were, so I knew who I had a chance with. For all I know one of the lads from 5ive or the Backstreet Boys could be too, but are secretly stuck in the same closet. *Surely what happened with Stephen wasn't a one-off, there must be another male pop star my age who's gay and who's just not saying it?* I feel frustrated and haven't even got success to take the edge off now, it seems to be dwindling by the day. If only people knew this happy-go-lucky pop star who sings about making them feel good, actually feels the complete opposite.

SMTV done, I grab my stuff and head out of the studio to find the car Virgin have sent to take me back to the hotel. A group of fans who have been waiting outside all morning in the cold are still gathered behind the barrier. I head over to say hello, always priding myself on treating them with respect and making their day. Even in my current low mood it takes nothing to give them a few minutes of my time.

'Are Steps still in there, Kav?' one of them asks.

'Not sure,' I reply, expecting a pic or at least an autograph request from the excitable crew. 'Will you go in and ask them to come out pleeeeease, we're freezin'.'

Not really the request I was hoping for.

'I have to go but I'm sure they will be out soon,' I answer, realising it's not me they're interested in.

I find the car and jump in. They've sent Mad Reggie, one of the more, shall we say, chatty drivers Virgin use. Reggie sounds like Fagin and looks like Nigel Havers on a budget. I hear through some reliable sources that he also serves up the odd gram of coke, about which I'm too nervous to inquire.

'Hello, Kavana. Regents Plaza, Maida Vale, son?'

Mad Reggie waits for me to confirm while I process that's the first time I've not been asked for as much as an autograph, never mind a pic.

'Sure!' I say, knowing that the only thing I'm really sure about is I will definitely be getting drunk tonight. Again. Maybe on the way back I'll drop a few hints to Reggie regarding doing some 'business' too. I could do with letting off some steam. Day off tomorrow anyway. No Sunday promo with this single. *T4* weren't interested and *Fully Booked* was, er, fully booked.

HUNG UP

I try to get to Manchester to see Mum and Dad and Mickey the cat as much as possible, mainly because I miss them and going up back home some weekends keeps me somewhat grounded. There's only so many parties or nights out at the Met Bar one can have without feeling like your soul is being sucked out along with your wallet. A night out for me could end up going a multitude of ways depending on the company I keep, and lately I seem to be drawn to those who lean towards the non-stop partying type of evening, which are usually dressed up to begin with a 'let's have dinner at Nobu'. I don't even like sushi, but sitting in a restaurant a few feet away from one of the Gallaghers or Kate Moss, in desperate hope I also get invited to the inner sanctum of Cool Britannia, does wonders for the ego. Not so much when you're back in your hotel room watching the ceiling with the birds tweeting with a paranoid coked-up empty soul and wallet to go with it. *Maybe one day*

I will get invited to Supernova Heights once I become
pals with them. I just need to prove that there's more to
me than what they think. Plus, I am also a northerner
so surely we would get on like a house on fire, hopefully
in Noel's £5 million one in Belsize Park.

Saturday night starts off in Manchester with Andrew
and I sitting in my bedroom at Mum and Dad's discussing
Wilson Phillips. When I had glandular fever in 1990 and
became housebound due to putting on two stone from
comfort eating (buttered toast and Coco Pops with hot
milk before bed anyone?) and God knows what else
this strange diagnosis did to a 13-year-old (and stone)
me, Andrew would come to visit me while I was off
school. I was at this time hating school anyway, due
to being mistaken for a girl on a daily basis and regularly
being called a poof, so my mysterious diagnosis could
not have come at a better time for me to not to have to
face these boy bullies, feeling like I was walking to the
guillotine every morning when entering the playground.
High school is no joke when you're a sensitive soul.
I managed to wangle a whole six months off school
thanks to easy parents and a strict application of talcum
powder on my face before coming down the stairs each
morning just to eke out the illness.

One of the comforts of this season of self-induced
agoraphobia in 1990 was the debut album of Wilson
Phillips. Something about those sweet Californian
harmonies and the slick Glen Ballard production (who
I would later stalk to produce me) seemed to heal me
like a big blanket of sunshine, which is just as well

since I was living like a teenage Count Dracula, fearing any daylight at all. The following year, now back at school, we went from buying albums on cassette and moved to the ultra-modern CD. One of Andrew's first purchases was Shakespears Sister's *Hormonally Yours* in HMV, while mine was, and with great excitement, the sophomore album by Wilson Phillips with the more edgier title *Shadows and Light*, with its slick black-and-white cover shot by legendary photographer Herb Ritts. Gone were the cowboy hats, denim and suede that my favourite country pop trio wore so well and in its place they were now in full glam couture, laughing knowingly to each other on the cover.

'I bet Carnie's the friendliest.'

'Oh, without a doubt, and I'd say she has a similar vocal tone to Bette Midler.'

'I do love all of them, though.'

'Aww, happy days.'

'I think they still do shows in Asia, and remember that video they were performing in China and getting mobbed, they were massive out there.'

'That was before Carnie had her stomach stapled. Was it stapled or did she just lose loads of weight?'

Whenever Andrew and I get together, it feels just like being a kid again. I'm just Anthony, the same one before all this happened, finding deep connection and joy with my best mate over teenage music fascinations.

It's good to be home.

The next day Andrew visits again and we go into the city centre for a few pints and a wander. After a mooch round the usual haunts we head back to mine in a black cab and order a curry. Dad's at home watching Sunday-night telly while Mum's out at bingo, Sunday night being the 'link up' where all the bingo halls link together to win the one big payout which can sometimes be in the thousands. I think she goes more for the entertainment factor and no doubt a chance to tell her gambling pals that her son's home visiting from his busy pop-star life in London. If only she knew.

While going through the local Indian takeaway menu upstairs in my room after rolling a joint to bring on the munchies even more, the phone rings.

UNKNOWN NUMBER.

A cold call from anyone is enough to give me high anxiety of the third kind, let alone the dreaded unknown number variety.

'Who the bloody hell is calling me at 7pm on a Sunday night on a bloody private number, are they mad?'

'Oh, just leave it, Anthony, you're always on the phone, they can leave a message,' says Andrew, knowing me well and that our time is precious, especially when you have Wilson Phillips to discuss. No doubt we will be moving on to the Reynolds Girls and Sonia next.

After not answering the private-numbered call, I hear a little ping, alerting me that whoever this Sunday-night disturber of my peace is also has the audacity to leave a bloody voicemail! *Don't they realise celebrities have private time too? What is wrong with some people?*

'Listen to it if you must, go on,' eye-rolls Andrew, knowing that my curiosity will not let me settle until I find out who the eager beaver and no doubt time-waster is. 'If you need to make an actual call, though, I'm not sitting here waiting as you're always on for ages. I'd rather go downstairs and watch bloody *Bullseye* with your dad than sit here with you rambling on.'

'I'm not making any calls! I just want to see what they want on a Sunday night! Hang on.'

I dial 123 and put the phone to my ear.

'Welcome to Orange mobile. You have one new message.'

'Hi, Kavana, this is Madonna calling. I'm here with someone you know and we were going to invite you to come join us at a party we're having tonight in London. You decided not to pick up, though, didn't you? So long, sucker.'

She doesn't call back.

A GAY OLD TIME

A wet gloomy November morning in Chalk Farm in 1998. I came to strange-sounding Chalk Farm on my first ever photo shoot in 1996 and genuinely expected cows and fields, not a bunch of warehouses and hipster cafés. I'm back a few times a month now, though, as it seems most of the mags use the warehouses in this area for shoots. Today I'm doing one with *Gay Times* magazine who are putting me on the cover. Considering I overthink most things, I must have somehow naively said yes to this not realising what it could entail. The fact that any magazine wants to put me on the cover is a miracle, but unlike the other mainstream gay mag *Attitude*, who asked me to be on theirs in August pre-'comeback' and is slightly more ambiguous and fashion-based, *Gay Times* will have me on the cover with the words GAY TIMES plastered above my head like a big neon sign drawing attention to my secret. Anxious how the interview will go, and what kinds of questions the journalist may ask, I've already got my guard up. I'm also lacking serotonin from the all-nighter I pulled again at the weekend when I ended up partying with two fashion types I found at the Met Bar and invited back for a knees-up at mine – aka, room 115 at the Regent's Plaza. One of them had a blunt fringe like Joan of Arc with a forehead so big I panicked every time she took her turn to do a line in fear of her abolishing the others that were racked out, and the other wouldn't shut up about her idol designer Isabella Blow, an ironic name given the way she was helping herself to the mini mountain of the very stuff I'd just paid for.

It feels like Virgin have thrown me to the wolves today. I'm out on a limb still with no guidance of what can and can't be said re my sexuality. I don't want to out myself, I'm not ready. I want to remain private but at the same time I, or we, need the cover feature to raise my profile. *Ugh.* It's almost like they are pushing me to say something by agreeing to this. *Do they know? Is it that obvious I'm gay? Why hasn't one single person in my professional world asked me?* Maybe giving me the invitation to talk about it could allow me to open up, but they either aren't bothered or are following my own clueless lead.

In walks Sam, our journalist for the day. High energy, twink-ish and pushing mid-thirties, Sam has an air of forced cheerfulness and a demeanour of being super-nice, but there's a sense it's a front, and he may possibly be crying inside from loneliness, so I feel for him, being lonely myself most of the time. Wanting to put him at ease and not come across in any way pop-starry, which I don't believe I am or ever have been, I am even more charming and northern and self-deprecating than normal and ask him lots of questions about himself to break the ice.

Sam doesn't bite, though, and everything I say he retaliates back with, 'How about you?!'

'Did you travel far, Sam?'

'Not really. How about you?!'

'Oh, I just came from the hotel.'

'It's alright for some, eh?!'

'This the first shoot of the day, then?'

'I've got a phoner with a HUGE name later, how about you?!'

Having had enough of the verbal ping-pong, and because this is not the dreaded interview yet, I quit while I'm ahead and go to hair and make-up (bit of powder and a wax of the curtains) and find an outfit to wear for the shoot from what stylist Dave sent via courier as it's Paris fashion week and he can't be in two places at once.

Sam carries on yapping away, this time to the photographer, where I can hear the words 'bare chest' and 'wind' being mentioned. *Eek.*

The shoot's actually a breeze, literally, as I stand in front of a large industrial fan with my chosen navy blue Dolce & Gabbana shirt flapping open. My hair had no need to be waxed as it now bounces in said wind with enough volume that I may as well be in a Timotei advert. A few dozen sultry poses later and it's a wrap, for the visuals at least.

As more grown-up interviews go, Sam seemed very sweet indeed. There were no real probing questions or gossipy undertones to his words, apart from one when he asked about my 'thoughts' on my gay fanbase, which considering I was talking to the biggest gay magazine in the UK seemed a silly question to what was going to be my clearly obvious answer – 'I love all my fans.'

Now this may have been an expected reply from, say, King of Pop Michael Jackson or another superstar, but since I may be heading to the Woolworths bargain bin in the not-too-distant future, I had to admit this was a mistake. It seems me trying to stay neutral on the gay thing may have just backfired and made me come across like an absolute prima donna of the most delusional kind. Another example of not thinking before I speak.

'That's perfect for now!' Sam says, stopping me from being able to somehow go back on my statement and attempt to make it less cringe.

'If we've missed anything out, we can maybe do a quick phoner, but I think we've got it all!'

I'm not buying it. I'm not exactly sure what he means by 'all' as I feel he was doing more talking than I was. Sam knows I'm gay, of course he bloody does, so this merry little interview dance we have just taken part in feels like a sham, just like all the others. Except this one is for the very readers that need someone to stand up and say, 'Pop stars my age are gay too!' I feel like a fraud but I'm sure it will be fine, I really need to trust people more. Plus, he's probably saving his more juicy questions for his seemingly much bigger star later on. Good luck with that, Sam.

* * *

Christmas comes and I get fat. The early onset of depression strikes on New Year's Day when the haunting bells on Band Aid's 'Do They Know it's Christmas?' ring out of Dad's wireless radio in the bathroom while I'm in the shower. Christmas songs seem pointless once it's over but this one in particular always seems to bring on the blues. My sister and brother-in-law have gone back to Cornwall and all festivities and family jollifications have come to an end. Mother is neurotic as ever but happy her son is home for the holidays. She isn't too happy about the net curtains in the front room stinking of cigarette smoke, though, due to me and my sister using the room for our soirées, which usually consist of just the two of us putting the world to rights over countless bottles of vino. For some bizarre reason 'Will You Wait For Me' has been a minor hit in Ireland, so Virgin put TV promo in for *The Late Late Show,* a chat show that goes out live every Friday night hosted by the beloved presenter and my father's favourite fellow Irishman, Gay Byrne. Speaking of Gay and my father (no, not that) I was more than a little mortified when Dad swanned in from his afternoon bookie's trip, proudly waving a big shiny copy of the very gay mag I did the interview for a few weeks back. They couldn't have chosen a more camp, seductive picture of me for the cover, and I was right, there in all its glory was my face (and half-opened shirt) with the big *Gay Times* logo above it.

'Look at this, son!' said Father, while I hoped the sofa would swallow me up in one. 'You're on *Gay*!'

Now, my father is an intelligent, well-read man (old Hollywood biographies mainly) but either I've misheard him, or he thinks the magazine is simply called *Gay* and that me allowing my face on the cover means that I am 'gay' too. I am yet to reveal anything regarding my sexuality to either parent so I need to think fast on what my reply is here. Do I correct him on the title of the mag? Like somehow adding the words *Times* to it completely throws off any scent that it's still a flaming-hot screaming gay magazine with his closeted son on the front.

'Oh Dad, don't be silly! It's called *Gay Times*, not *Gay*, ha! Anyway, how was the bookies? Any football on tonight?'

GAME OVER

May, 1999

'Mr Conroy will see you now,' says the new receptionist I don't recognise at Virgin Records' offices. The day I have feared happening has finally arrived. After the lacklustre reception to my supposed big comeback I have been called into the office of Virgin Records HQ to discuss 'next steps' re my career, which also means my life. It seems even though my new album has done extremely well in Southeast Asia and other far-off territories, I have a feeling these so-called next steps are in no uncertain terms going to be the chop. Walking down the aisle past all the departments of the record company workers I have now become friends with over the last few years feels more like walking to the guillotine to meet my executioner.

'It's been an absolute pleasure working with you at Virgin. You really are beloved by a lot of people here.'

My stomach drops and I feel my heart beating fast

in my chest. It doesn't help that behind Paul Conroy, MD of Virgin Records, is an array of gold discs from the million-selling artists that are also beloved by the workers here. All that team effort and success laughing back at me just to rub it in. I'm about to be locked out of the club, and it hurts.

'It's just that we have obviously had some big changes at the label.'

Oh? Maybe I've got it wrong? He's right, there have been some big changes, huge in fact. For example, my original A&R woman is on maternity leave and the man who signed me is too busy living it up in LA, reaping what he sowed with the Spice Girls, which in effect leaves me with none of my original cheerleaders. My heart rate slows down and I wonder if he's about to tell me something more hopeful. Maybe he's realised all I need is a new A&R after my depressing meeting prior to this one with Joanne's replacement, a Scottish man with a Paul Weller haircut and a pair of Clarks Wallabees who was more interested in blowing his own trumpet re: The Verve's recent huge comeback than hearing me cling on for dear life with suggestions of what my next steps could be. Maybe Mr Conroy has come to his senses and realised that with all the success I've had in Asia that I too should in fact be sent out to the States just like the Spice Girls and be given the push I've always wanted out there? My music has always sounded more US-radio-friendly anyway. Even the Los Angeles office over there really championed my record but were forced to go with pop pals 911 due to the wave of boy bands having successes everywhere. They ended up being on the soundtrack to *Casper the Ghost* while I disappeared off their radar.

'Please excuse me, Kav. Sorry, one moment.'

Mr Conroy takes an important call that's been sent through. I notice he said 'sorry' too, which means he respects me. Wants to impress me and keep me on his side. *Phew*. I sometimes wonder how I can go from thinking my life is over to seeing myself having hits on the Billboard Hot 100. Talk about extreme! *I really need to start thinking more positively. I must get back into reading* The Power of Now. *Starting today.*

'Sorry about that, so where were we?'

I sit back and cross my legs, placing my hand underneath my chin to show how focused and interested I am, a bit like George Michael in the 'Fast Love' video, brooding yet confident, master of my destiny, that kind of thing.

Beloved and next steps. Beloved and next steps. Beloved and next steps, going round like a mantra in my mind.

'Oh yes, so there's no easy way of saying this but we will be letting you go as of today.'

'Go where?' I say, hearing my own voice, which sounds suddenly like a child's.

I'd never had a real drunk blackout, never mind a sober one, but I don't remember much after that apart from the noise of phones, faxes, success – the sounds that filled me with excitement and wonder when I first arrived at these offices now filled me with a hollow dread and shock.

Everything I think I know about my place in the world has changed. I walk out of Virgin Records for the last time. I call my manager Pete who seems to already have an inkling of what happened, but as always is as kind and hopeful as he can be.

'We've all given it our best go, mate. It's just really hard and it's a tough industry right now. Let's grab a coffee and figure out what's next.'

With all of his well-meaning intentions and genuine sincerity, I can hear in his voice that he knows we've run out of options. Us sitting in Café Rouge on the Albert Bridge by his office figuring out what they could be would be enough to make me want to jump.

'Thanks, Pete, I think I just need some time to think about it.'

I hang up and keep walking. It doesn't help that it's raining right on cue, just to add extra cinematic effect to what feels like my world-ending news. I walk and walk and walk in the rain, my little brain for once unable to compute what just happened. Past the posh eateries in Chelsea and over the Thames, a contrast to my misery and the rain that's now soaked through my smart blazer I wore as a last chance saloon pick, to make an impression with Mr Conroy. *Oh wait, he's wearing a blazer, I say! Blimey, we must keep him on!* No such luck. I carry on squelching along the bridge until I find the nearest pub. I go in and order a pint, the barmaid, seeing how drenched I am, offering me a towel, which I think may be for the pots judging by the fact it was on the floor by the sink at her feet. I take it and give myself a rub. Feeling washed-up has a whole new sense of meaning.

WESTVIEW TOWERS

Hollywood, August, 2001

My father has cancer. Bowel. They may need to remove it. Colostomy bag for the rest of his life. Dad says he would rather let it spread than have a bag. Too proud. My dad. The man who will wear a shirt and tie just to go to the bookies. Always smart. A Dublin Dean Martin. Smells like Wrigley's chewing gum and Old Spice aftershave. Always smiling. Nah. No way. It can't be. I find out the news over the phone with my sister while having my Earl Grey tea in my new Pottery Barn mug while staring at the Hollywood sign which is to the left of my balcony on my new rented condo in an exclusive building called 'Westview Towers' – which has valet for the car I don't have and a concierge for the visitors I'm yet to meet – overlooking Sunset Boulevard. I am shocked and gutted and feel helpless being so far away. The issue with this news about my possibly dying father is that I've just moved here on a three-year

O-1 visa for people with 'extraordinary talent' and a few thousand dollars to show for it. Is it disgusting and selfish that my second thought is about my career and that my dreams of cracking America could be threatened by it? Not the best timing, is it? Just as I start to feel some real freedom and hope, this happens. *Please, God, let him be OK.*

The family all agree I must not rush home and that until they find out more I need to stay focused and try not to worry. It's easier said than done, though. How can I parade myself around this town meeting agents and producers and God knows who else Jonny the entertainment lawyer has set up meetings with, and be on full extraordinarily talented form knowing my beautiful, kind father is about to die or be forced to wear a bag on his waist for the rest of his life? I decide to get on a plane home. They seem out of their depth with it all. Rattling around in house number two that I've now somehow bought for them after the one I bought outright after the council house is deemed too small and my financial advisor suggested it was a good idea to invest in a bigger property. I fly home and I need to be the good son. I need to be there for my mum and dad. I need a drink.

Thankfully my father's cancer is treatable, and by a miracle they manage to join his bowel back together without having to give him a colostomy bag. We are all saved and there is hope on the horizon. I stay in Manchester for a month while he returns from hospital to recuperate. It's hard to come back to LA, but Dad insists I must. He won't allow me to not follow my dream and, even though I am riddled with guilt, I do head back promising to make regular visits home. *I will make it my priority. It's only a 10-hour flight, really. I hope I'm making the right decision. I just have to give this stateside opportunity a chance, not just for me but for all of us.* It's not like I didn't try to make stuff happen in the UK, and even though Virgin did end up having to pay me £50,000 to leave the label and hand over the master to my song 'Will you Wait for Me' which I can now release in the US – thanks to an oversight over the option on my third album – with nothing happening at home and no manager wanting to touch me, I'd go through that money in no time. At least I can see it as an investment in LA where I have a clean slate and new exciting and powerful connections.

* * *

March 2002

Crunch Fitness is the gym where all the famous people go so I join. It's important to network, so why not kill two birds with one stone? I trained at Crunch Fitness with Greg on my first jaunt to Los Angeles so it seems fitting to get my very own membership and come here to do my cross-training (back fat) and weights (arms and chest). I don't bother with legs as they can do for now. On my third day at Crunch I spotted none other than Matt Goss, Heath Ledger and also Debbie Gibson in a leotard (Debbie, not Matt or Heath). I definitely caught eyes with Debbie by the free weights but she was mid working out with her PT, plus what was I going to say? 'Oh, hi, Debbie, I was a teen pop star too, and like you write my own songs but no one really saw my talent either. "Electric Youth" is a classic!' Hardly. New cool movie star on the block Heath was going through the motions with his PT in a beanie hat, while Matt, on the other hand, I had a real opportunity to talk to, but was too nervous. It did feel weird being a few feet away from the man who sang 'When Will I Be Famous?' and had a nation of Brosettes adoring him like a real pop star. I just assumed he may see me as competition now I'm on his turf. He's obviously come out here to make it too after his flame dimmed in the UK, so doesn't need me raining on his parade.

Westview Towers also has other actors and famous-ish residents. I saw a man from *Melrose Place* in the lift yesterday who said 'Howdy' rather than hello. I'm back in touch with Greg and, after a few drinks at the Standard Hotel on Saturday night we ended up going back to Kimberly (daughter of Rod) Stewart's penthouse on the top floor and hung out. I have also made friends with a rather blunt (just like her fringe) German hairstylist to the stars called Katja who works at Vidal Sassoon on Rodeo Drive. I met her at a nightclub called Deux and she offered me free haircuts whenever I choose! She also styles the daughters of Ozzy and Sharon Osbourne who she tells me are fans of mine, WTF?! I wonder if I could be a series regular on their reality show *The Osbournes* which is huge out here. I ask her to put in a good word. Every angle and opportunity must be looked at if I'm going to succeed in this town.

I'D RATHER JACK

'Jack! So great to see you again! I'll read for the part of Susan, so whenever you're ready,' greets the Casting Director sat behind a pop-up table and chair in an empty car park in a sweltering hot Studio City.

I've had a callback for one of the very first auditions my new commercial agent Robyn has sent me on. Because I'm not a celebrity over here just yet, I can put myself out there not just for movie roles but commercials too, as the latter pay big bucks and until I hit the big time, 'a booking is a booking, honey!' as Robyn likes to tell me. Today's possible 'booking' is for a late night 'cult' (i.e. audience of five) soap opera called *Undressed* and it's on MTV. I decide to go for 'Jack Kavanagh' for all my acting auditions with that being my father's birth name. The casting director has no idea that my name is in fact Anthony, Kav or Kavana depending on who I'm talking to, but I had to choose yet another identity as there is already an Anthony Kavanagh in Equity over here. No biggie though, I quite like the rebrand and it could have a ring to it when I'm at the Oscars. The role in question on the soap is for 'Jonny', a British student at the high school where the episode takes place, who in return for getting some of his fellow female students to do his homework will teach them about the birds and the bees, so to speak, involving a scene with one student in question, Susan, where they make out in the back of a bus. *Gulp.*

Having not had an audition of any kind in a long time I am surprised that they have asked to see me again, as I fluffed my lines the first time and am yet to correct them when they said, 'Oh, we love your Australian accent!' Today, though, I am word-perfect and feel that I may just have this in the can, judging by the expression on the face of the casting director reading for the part of Susan who blushed at my confidence and cool Aussie charm when I leaned in cheekily at the end and took it upon myself to say, 'I guess we aren't doing the kiss today, then?!'

'Would you mind re-reading it in a posher, say, British accent? Like Hugh Grant maybe?!' chuckles the casting lady.

'Of course!' I reply, this being music to my ears. 'Maybe we should add a "whoops-a-daisy" while we are at it? Make him more witty. How about a cheeky glance at the camera to break the fourth wall?!' I say, now directing the woman in charge, like a young, overenthusiastic Jeremy Irons in a regional workshop of *Godspell.*

With the scene(s) wrapped, I head out into the hazy warm LA evening. I love the city at night, it reminds me of what I used to see in the movies as a kid or in TV shows where you'd see the characters holding brown paper bags with their groceries, just like I do now. My phone vibrates in my pocket. It's Robyn. I booked the job. My first big break in the City of Angels. My dad was right, I needed to give this a good shot. Things are really starting to happen. I head over to Whole Foods and get some turkey mince and pasta sauce, minus the pasta. *I'll need to cut out all carbs until filming day. Just the one of bottle of wine tonight too. Empty calories.*

* * *

Months pass quickly and I make another trip to the UK to see how Dad is getting on and how Mum is coping. Dad's doing better than any of us could have imagined, taking himself to his weekly chemo appointments at the hospital on the bus and not complaining once about it. Mum has taken it in her stride too, doing what she can with the skills she has, and still cooks the boil-in-the-bag fish in butter sauce with boiled potatoes that go into a 'lob' in the pan, as she calls them if she forgets to turn the gas down in time.

It's surreal being home, and I can't help but feel a sense of guilt that I'm not there. It's one thing paying your parents' mortgage but in my heart of hearts I know they'd prefer to have me back living in the council house with them. I take taxis everywhere when I'm home, checking in with old pals and telling them of my Hollywood escapades with them sat open-mouthed at my antics, such as partying at the *Playboy* mansion where I did too much coke and had to be hosed down in a gold shower room by one of Mr Hefner's *Playboy* bunnies (a snippet I obviously leave out for Mum and Dad), or the wild parties I get invited to in the Hollywood Hills at movie producers' houses, necking Ecstasy in hot tubs with A-listers and their hangers-on (another part best left out for the folks). What I don't report back, though, is how lonely I'm starting to feel and that I'm worried I may have made a mistake but am too caught up in the whirlwind of it all to come home. Or that when I'm not partying with whichever new group of Hollywood 'friends' I've met randomly in the VIP of my locals, The Standard or The Viper Room, I'm usually on a comedown, eating pizza while watching *The Tonight Show* and feeling sad that I'm nowhere near getting to be on there myself.

It's been almost a year since I moved to LA and the only thing to write home about is my small part in two episodes of a soap opera (watched by late-night stoned American students) and a few demos of songs I've paid for myself that aren't really cutting it as far as sounding like hits. It's not all doom and gloom, though. My old manager Pete has set up his own music publishing label and wants to sign me as a writer. Even though the label is UK-based and I live out in LA, he still believes that it would work and that I could write some possible hits with some more established writers. The thought of writing for other artists doesn't exactly fill my creative soul with joy, but it's not done Cathy Dennis any harm. It would also get me in the room with some big guns and I could keep the demos we write, which I will most likely sing on, and they can pitch them to whoever they feel like while I can use them to shop my own US deal, so it's a potential win-win. *I could get a record deal AND get a cut for Celine Dion while I'm at it!*

GOLDEN INVITE

LA, 2003

'How do you fancy an all-expenses paid trip to perform for the Prince of Brunei?'

Apart from replying to ask whether he wonders if I know what religion the Pope is, I reply a big fat YES to Pete's request. He's now formally my music publisher but still gets the odd UK request come in for me from when he was my manager, which so far has only been a panto in Southend and an advert for a driving school. Considering I'm now living on the other side of the Atlantic and I can't drive, we passed on both. The offer in question today, Pete tells me, while I'm sweating on a machine in Gold's Gym in West Hollywood (Crunch was by now too expensive), is from Prince Azim, the son of the Sultan of Brunei and a loyal pop music fan. I became friendly with the prince after he came backstage with his hefty security and pals on the last *Smash Hits* tour. A cheeky and delightful character, the prince wants me to perform at his birthday party in Brunei and will fly myself and a guest out there for an all-expenses paid trip and provide a hefty sum in cash. Pete also tells me that to make it authentic, he will have the actual set from *Top of the Pops* flown in for my tiny little gig in the palace.

'Well, it's a yes, obviously! But they do know I'm in LA, right? And that I'll have to fly from here?' I ask, forgetting we are dealing with one of the richest people in the world and what the prince wants, the prince gets.

'Course, mate. You'll have to change at Paris, I think. You OK with that?'

'Er, yeah?!'

'OK, mate. Leave it with me and we will get back to you with an itinerary. You just need to make sure you take someone responsible with you.'

'Oh sure, yes. I've got a good idea who that will be. Let me check and I'll get back ASAP.'

With that I hang up the phone. I don't even have to think who my plus-one will be – I have to ask Greg. Not only is he well-travelled and great company, he looks like a bloody film star too. Those bloody royals will love him. I call him but it goes straight to voicemail. He's probably putting some poor actress through her paces in the gym.

'Yo, Greg, it's meeeeee! Call me back as soon as you're done. Wanna come meet a prince?'

* * *

I've burned my finger on the grill in the yard at Greg's while he shoots some basketball hoops with a middle-aged actor client who looks like he will soon pass out. I'm making sirloin beef burgers from Trader Joe's food hall as I need some protein after my workout class at Gold's, where I also nearly passed out. Due to my burned finger I run into Greg's kitchen and pop two Advil (American ibuprofen, apparently) and slug it down with some chilled Fiji water from the fridge. I hesitate to run my burned finger under the tap as I always think cold water makes the sting worse the second you take it away. I go back to where the Advil is to get some ice, only to realise it wasn't Advil I took, it was Ephedrine, a fucking intense heavy-duty caffeine and God-knows-what-else-is-in-it pill that Greg must have forgotten he put in his gym studio medical cabinet where he keeps all his other lotions and potions. All above board and certified by the US fitness standards but when I enquired about them before Greg said, 'No, dude. Those guys will fuck you up!'

So now not only do I have a sizzling finger but my heart rate and anxiety could go through the roof due to the amount of caffeine inside these pre-workout monster pills – just in time for my power lunch with my new film and TV agents this afternoon in Beverly Hills.

PLANET HOLLYWOOD

Greed. Me. You. Hello. Mickey. Metal mickey,
I'm going places. Sometimes I wonder what it's
all about, Alfie. I'm going. If you please. Stay
strong. Hope fails. KANSAS. Gluttony. Wise
man. Wise woman. Oprah. Toby jug. Non-
stop masturbating. Every day is like Sunday
and Monday and Tuesday. Many chats. Yoga.
No order. Cellphone. Mr Cellophane. No. Do
it. When will it begin? I'm NOT LONELY.
I miss my mum and dad. I'm happy! Stop
wine. Sunshine. Discipline. I'm so lucky. I am
powerful. I must believe. Superstar. Hell. Lucky
me. Worzel! Glo Worm. Hi, I'm Anthony. Fuck.
Is this really supposed to help me?

I'm not having much luck so far with this 'morning pages' routine, an exercise where you're supposed to write a few pages every morning of anything and everything that comes to mind without fear or self-consciousness, suggested by the book I bought called *The Artist's Way* by a lady called Julia Cameron, who according to the blurb on the back is an author, poet and self-help guru. Just as well it's for my eyes only as if anyone read the outpouring of my morning thoughts then they may have me committed. According to my new friend Annie from acting class, this book is a must for all aspiring creatives to help gain access to their true potential and creativity, which is something I've been lacking. Coming up with new songs in the studio and nailing these acting auditions takes more than just looking good and having a 'cute' British accent, it seems.

I met Annie on the first day of enrolling at acting coach Susan Batson's Masterclass. Susan is a force to be reckoned with and looks like Chaka Khan with a touch of Eartha Kitt, with an attitude of both to match, and wants every emotion out on the table every Thursday morning in her mirrored studio on Hollywood and Vine. On the first day we had to stand in a circle to begin and one at a time go forth into the middle and dance in front of the rest of the group. First up was a small impish girl called Becks, who seemed to be wearing pyjamas but didn't ever say why. She also had a baseball cap on which said 'Badass Bitch' on the front, but judging by the way she danced in the circle gave more the impression she stayed in her bedroom most nights watching *Dawson's Creek*. This was not the case with Annie, however, who went from appearing to be quite shy to walking slowly to the centre and erupting into what can only be described as a sex-starved whirling dervish who was simultaneously giving birth to Satan. With tight ginger curls and piercing blue eyes, Annie is obsessed with Princess Diana and anything royal-family related, even though she thinks they are lizards. She is also one of the first students at UCLA to be doing a masters in 'Positive Psychology', a new course on the power of the mind. I went up to her after our first class and told her how I admired how she allowed herself to be so 'vulnerable' in the circle exercise that morning, which she thanked me for. I then made the mistake of asking her if anyone had ever told her she looked like a young Sissy Spacek, to which she replied, 'Fuck you, asshole.' Since then we speak every day.

I've been renting the attic room in Greg's shared bachelor pad since I couldn't justify the rent on my apartment at Westview Towers *and* keep up the mortgage payments on Mum and Dad's house in Manchester. Greg's house is on Hollywood Boulevard and its original owner was actress Carole Lombard. The star was married to Clark Gable and died in a plane crash on her way back from performing for the troops in the 1940s, and there's framed pictures of her in the dining room where she once held court with her infamous dinner parties.

I'm surprised Greg is forever single as he has the looks of a male model, but it seems he has no interest in the majority of the girls in Hollywood. This works highly in my favour, as I don't have to pretend I'm on the lookout for a hot female date either. I know Greg wouldn't judge me or care at all if I confessed that I was gay but I just can't, yet. I also need to be a little more aware of the fact that Greg trains his clients at his home gym set-up in what was Carole's old guest house. I certainly wasn't expecting to bump into Gavin Rossdale from Bush post-workout in the yard while I was reaching for the almond creamer from the fridge yesterday. He seemed a little surprised to see a British pop star with wild hair in boxer shorts parading around the kitchen. *Saying that, he didn't actually ask me what I did, but I had a feeling he recognised me. Delusional of me maybe, but I did feel there was some kind of a 'knowing' between us, like when two famous people at party who have never actually met pass each other and their eyes meet – like a 'I'm also in the fame club and I see you'. Either that or Gavin just fancies me. I did hear he allegedly had an affair with Boy George's mate Marilyn back in the day, so maybe he's bisexual? Thing is, I daren't ask Greg as then he will know I'm interested. We could never date, though, as he's happily loved up with Gwen Stefani and Greg trains her too . . .*

* * *

I've taken the wrong escalator in the Beverly Center shopping mall. This one will take me out at the pet shop and I want Bloomingdale's for a change. Petco was a novelty at first but there's only so many chihuahuas

I can play with through the glass on a daily basis and not look deranged. I just can't help myself going there for some reason. Who am I kidding? I know exactly the reason. I'm bored. I have a little more time on my hands than I expected, and puppies give me joy. I'm not exactly hustling between appointments like when I first arrived, and although I've had auditions I've still only got the soap opera I booked the same month I arrived as the main credit on my acting CV. Well, that and my other credit being 'Appearance' in *Spice World: The Movie* where in the dressing-room scene my pop pals and labelmates put my Virgin Records promo pic on the wall before filming as a laugh. It made the cut, so it's an 'Appearance' nonetheless, and so far no casting directors checked.

On the music side, my new 'co'-manager Peter is still full of beans and optimistic even though we are on our second demo package to present to US labels. I signed with Gold Mountain Entertainment after the attorney I hired put me in touch with manager Ron Stone who has guided the careers of Beastie Boys, Nirvana, Beck and Belinda Carlisle, to name a few on his roster, so not only was I overjoyed to be offered representation but I hoped I was in good hands. But since not much happened on the first round of demos we presented, charismatic and silver-haired Mr Stone has gently passed me over to Peter Shurkin ('Like Gherkin'), his young and eager assistant. Peter, who looks like a young emo Woody Allen, knows I can write decent songs and sees my ambition, but now agrees that the blue-eyed pop-soul thing is a bit dated. Me referencing George Michael as a career trajectory isn't cutting it either. Big Manager Ron has an up-and-coming artist called Rufus Wainwright who not only plays piano while singing but is boldly, openly gay to boot.

'You can totally play piano, maybe we should go down the Rufus route with a pop edge,' exclaimed Peter, over two 'double-doubles' at In-N-Out Burger. I admire his chutzpah, it gives me hope, but there's an underlying concern with the statement, as I wonder if Peter was somehow hinting at me being 'out' like Rufus? He can't mean that, surely, as he has no idea re my private life, so I agreed, craftily making more emphasis on the me-playing-piano part being the new angle we should try. We decided on some intimate showcases around town – just me and an electric keyboard should be the next port of call.

'It worked for Elton at the Troubadour!' I said, delighted at how quick my brain thought up such an iconic and ballsy comparison.

'Hell, yeah! Let me look at some venues!' It wasn't just the burger Peter bit. Maybe the blind are leading the blind, but it's another ray of hope to cling to for now.

* * *

I look out of the box window slurping my coffee, staring at the bougainvilleas on the front lawn. The same lawn where former owner Carole Lombard threw her wacky parties for film-land's elite. I can see it now – Natalie

Wood stubbing out a cigarette while slurping her Scotch and soda, Clark Gable flirting with one of the young production assistants from MGM. What a time to be alive. Who'd have thought I'd end up living here in actual Hollywood in an old movie star's house? I've come a long way from Moston. Had I not overheard the woman from the Taiwanese record label calling me fat (or 'pang zi', which means 'little plump') I may have never started this whole chain of events to get me here and meet Greg. That and having a dream of wanting something bigger for myself. Real respect and acclaim in an industry that appreciates *real* talent. Now, with my new American lease of life, I want Grammys and Oscars. I want it all and I will get it all. I believe the universe conspires to make life happen exactly the way we desire it to. We just have to believe in it. I believe in it, and I believe there's a bigger plan at hand, and I just need to focus and stay positive.

* * *

'Belvedere Martini, straight up. No vermouth.' I'm sat in the hotel bar of the Chateau Marmont on Sunset Boulevard at noon. It's overcast in Hollywood and I'm feeling antsy, which means a little vodka is required. Daytime drinking is happening a bit more often than I'd like to admit, but I'm sure things will pick up soon so I'm enjoying my downtime while I can. I've arranged to meet Annie here to discuss our TV pilot idea. The concept being a British musician/actor (me) and an up-and-coming actress (her) finding their way in a town like this, while they try to hit the big time. We have decided to call it *Grit* because that's what it takes to make it in this town, and boy don't we know it. What I haven't revealed to Annie yet is that I've had a callback for a TV show my agent has put me up for. *Rock Star: INXS* – where 15 contestants will compete to become the lead vocalist of INXS, who have reformed since the passing of original frontman Michael Hutchence. Ridiculous boots to fill but the show has been greenlit by Mark Burnett, the biggest producer in town, and it's for CBS, *and* David Geffen is involved. This means it's sure to be huge. The winner will be the new frontman/woman of the group and record an album followed by a world tour. Being in a huge rock band was not on the cards, but hey! Here's hoping Mr Geffen doesn't recognise me from when I went as a plus-one to his house party in the hills a couple of months ago, as it was wall-to-wall gay Hollywood and I want to remain private at least until I make it. On the other hand, perhaps it will work in my favour?

WRONG BITCH

Pacific Palisades, 2005

Middle eights can be annoying. That part of the song that comes after the second chorus but doesn't always. Not *all* songs have one, you see. Some songs have no middle eight at all. Some songs think they are too cool for the middle eight. I am still on the fence, as whether you're writing the song alone or as a co-writer the need for one depends on the style of song, and as far as I'm concerned they can sound a little self-indulgent. A bit try-hard. No one wants that.

Today's writing session is with a songwriter I am working with called Michelle, and we are currently deciding if our guitar-pop song, that didn't exist an hour ago and now miraculously does, does in fact require the infamous middle eight. Michelle is an LA songwriter and former artist herself and is warmer than warm, and even for LA standards a little kooky. Short pixie-cut hair and mid-thirties, Michelle has big brown eyes and reminds me of Demi Moore in *Ghost*, which may be a little overfamiliar to mention just yet. I have a tendency to overshare and not every thought needs to be uttered when first meeting someone, like an excitable puppy desperate to be liked. We are sat cross-legged on the floor in her modest studio out the back of her and her husband's Sylvanian Families woodland-style house. When I was discussing possible co-writers with the A&R woman from EMI Publishing over here, she reeled off a list of hit songwriters she knew, name-checking that some had Grammy awards and some Billboard Hot 100s, some were connected to Clive Davis with number ones from the past, and she would approach them on my behalf and see who would be interested.

GRAMMY AWARDS.

CLIVE DAVIS.

BILLBOARD HOT 100.

I'M EXACTLY WHERE I'M MEANT TO BE.

So far I've written with Oliver Leiber, son of Elvis hit-maker Jerry Leiber, Patrick Leonard who wrote 'Like a Prayer' with Madonna and now Michelle. The only small problem I'm having is that I'm not exactly sure what she has written due to getting my wires crossed and being overwhelmed with the meetings my film agent is also sending me on. *Am I running myself into the ground by attempting both, or should I just choose one profession and stick to it? Movie star or pop star? I may as well throw everything against the wall and see what sticks.* I'm finding it a bit difficult to concentrate today, though, as I have somehow convinced myself that Michelle has written the song 'Bitch' by Meredith Brooks due to that style of song being somehow thrown in the mix at my publishing meeting (the current trend of hit songs over here is guitar pop with a scratchy beat. Think 'Complicated' by Avril Lavigne and you get the gist). *But what if she didn't and I congratulate her on it and make a huge faux pas? I must also not call her 'Meredith' as her name is Michelle, but the M is confusing.*

Before I can dig deeper, Michelle stands up and then flops straight down into what I know to be a downward-dog yoga position that I saw the instructor do in my first ever yoga class at the weekend. Michelle exhales deep breaths and groans before rounding off with another pose, tucking her knees underneath her and dramatically placing her forehead on the ground.

'Mmm, if only we could just exist in child's pose . . . Bliss!' she says while I pretend to scribble lyrics, wondering what to reply. I slurp the dregs of my Starbucks iced mocha instead, making bubble noises through the straw.

'Another coffee?'

'Sure.'

'Old milk or almond?'

'Oh, I'm easy. I really don't mind.'

Michelle slides into her camel-coloured Birkenstocks while hiking up her yoga leggings, to reveal a camel of another type we hadn't bargained for, and disappears into the house humming our new tune. Her big Labrador Jessie, who barked and lovingly pounced at me on the way in, comes to greet me with his big yellow bushy tail, knocking over an incense burner followed by a cactus plant in the corner. So LA.

I find it weird that she asked me if I wanted old milk. *Must be some new LA health fad. Something to do with that good bacteria for the stomach they talk about. Should have said almond.*

HOLLYWOOD CHARLES

Audition after audition and not a bite. It seems the soap opera was an anti-climax and a cruel joke from the gods of fame to land me a role so soon in my LA adventure. It now seems like a distant memory and I'm yet to book a commercial either. The closest I got of late was a callback for a Blockbusters ad that required an English accent, and they went for the American guy who was putting one on. It didn't help that I blacked out the day before after one too many frozen margaritas at the Standard Hotel on Sunset, falling asleep in the shallow end of the pool and coming to in a stranger's hotel room who wasn't even there. It's that moment when I realise that I may be at the beginning of an addiction which will insidiously follow and baffle me for years to come, but I keep on 'dabbling' at the weekends, hanging out with my new friends in Hollywood at various clubs and parties across town.

It's at one of these parties that I meet Charles, an older

man from New York who came to LA after crashing and burning on Wall Street in the eighties and losing everything, 'Manhattan penthouse, the lot', culminating in him becoming homeless and living barefoot in Central Park. These days Charles is an artist who is in and out of recovery. He goes to 12-step meetings 'when I feel I need them', he tells me, a term I will latch on to when it also suits me in the future. My new friend is clearly going through his phase of 'not needing them' at the moment, as he is currently telling me about 'ice', a party drug he loves that gives him 'total fucking clarity' apparently, allowing him to work on his sculptures for sometimes days at a time.

'Wanna get out of here and do some?'

I profess how, as an artist myself, I also could do with this creative and inspiring wonder drug and that maybe we could even create some art together.

'You could sit for me while I sculpt you,' he says. 'I also have a seven-inch African wooden bongo set we can jam on.'

Christ.

Rather than say, 'Maybe another time,' we head back to Charles's place, feeling lit from the strong vodkas as I start to recognise that all-too-familiar craving for narcotics course through me. It doesn't really matter what it entails, as long as I get a hit, even if that means sitting like a statue while banging on some drums.

Once we get to Charles's apartment he shows me round and then we sit cross-legged on two giant bean-bags. He reaches into his pocket to present the 'ice', which looks like coke but rockier, as in little crystals. The wiser part of me knows what this stuff is – crystal meth, also known as 'Tina' – but I'm happy to play dumb, as not only have I always wanted to try this but now it's within reach the greedy addict in me wants it as soon as possible.

Charles puts some of the stuff in a glass pipe with a ball at the end and begins to light it from underneath, and the ball end slowly fills with white smoke. He then places the pipe part towards my lips and says 'suck', which I do, then breathe in the smoke all the way down my throat into my lungs and follow his instructions to 'hold it in'. I feel a warm rush of chemical bliss in my brain like something I've never experienced before. Not even the feeling of E can compare to whatever this stuff is doing to me and now my chest. A euphoria sent from the heavens, I am touched by God himself and within seconds of him taking back the pipe I am higher than I've been in my life. It's a different high, though – this is no sloppy loved-up hazy feeling like E and it's different from the teeth-grinding confidence boost from coke. This has a mellow edge while at the same time makes you feel like you could take over the world. Not to mention horny. Like I could fuck this very beanbag I'm perched on, never mind Charles.

Twenty-four hours later I leave the place a twisted paranoid wreck with eyes like pins. *I will never touch the stuff again,* I swear to myself.

BLACKOUTS AND HOT DOGS

Money is an issue. A big one. Me pretending to my folks that everything is going wonderfully here in Hollywood is doing me no favours. Neither is the time zone of when I call home. I get so nervous some days about having to put on a good front that I have to sink a few beers to put me in a good mood so they don't hear it in my voice. With the eight-hour time difference they are usually just rising while I'm on my third cold Heineken (bought in eight packs from Wholefoods obviously), any later than that and I'm wasted and sometimes even forget what I've said the previous time we spoke. It's like memory loss or amnesia – whole conversations just erased from my memory the next day. I thought 'blacking out' meant literally that, but it seems you actually still function. I've started to realise this a bit more when Dad asked how the 'movie premiere with

Elizabeth Taylor' went, which was a total over-the-top drunken lie that I must have concocted to make myself sound busy.

I express some of my financial worries to my accountant Sandra back in the UK who also seems to be a bit sozzled on the phone call, even if it is only 2pm in London. She tells me not to worry and that, 'You're going to make it, hen! I just know my Kavstar is gonna be huge out there!' Kavstar is a new name she has adopted for me, instead of 'my pop star' and I'm not sure which one is worse or, more to the point, which one of us is more delusional regarding me making it, me or her.

My friend Keanu (not that one) I met in acting class, upon hearing my financial concerns, offers me a part-time job on his father's hot-dog stand in downtown LA. Although I'm a little embarrassed it is a much better plan than having to work in retail or be a server at, say, The Cheesecake Factory, which is what a few other out-of-work stars-in-the-making seem to be doing. I'm also not sure bar work would be a good idea as I'd be too tempted to drink on the job. So this offer actually sounds ideal. Downtown LA is out of the way and no one will see me. It will pay me a couple of hundred dollars cash a week. I can cycle there (yes, the cost of taxis was becoming unaffordable so I bought a bike) and do what seems an easy job outside in the sunshine, so I'll get a tan and some exercise in the process.

'You will love it, dude! Plenty of that sweet Latina pussy too,' he says. Keanu is another one I'm yet to tell of my sexual leanings, and with him being an up-and-coming actor also, and being straight, I felt it best to leave that part out.

'Great!' I say, realising that something has to give, and I can't pawn any more jewellery, including the Cartier watch that's been sitting there at the pawn shop on Sunset Strip since August and now it's January. 'When will I start? I mean, er, what will I do?'

I'm yet to tell Keanu that I haven't done work like this since my one and only job at McDonald's, which went tits up, and although I'm sure shoving a sausage in some bun rolls is pretty easy I will need some kind of briefing of what it entails.

'Meet me outside Hotel Cecil at 11am tomorrow, OK? We go from there.'

I wasn't entirely convinced at Keanu's parting words of 'We go from there,' but needs must so I head out there the next morning, bleary-eyed and yet bushy-tailed after a late night with my friend Versa, a Greek red-haired goddess of a woman from London who has her own PR company aptly named Gorgeous on Melrose. Versa is one of my more 'real' friends and a delight to be around – an older, wiser sister who has witnessed a few of my drunken antics of late and raised concerns along with some other 'real' friends. I didn't tell her about my new job today, though, as she would never have allowed me to hold her hostage at the Snake Pit bar confessing my woes until the wee hours about 'not making it yet'.

I park my bike round a fire hydrant downtown after

a wild goose chase of finding this hotel named Cecil, which looks like something out of an Alfred Hitchcock movie, and I soon realise that I have hit Skid Row. Not like that (just yet, anyway) but actual, literal Skid Row, the place I've only ever heard about in movies or late-night news channels or via that scary rock band with big hair from the eighties. Streets lined with trash and tent after tent lined up alongside dirty makeshift shelters, not to mention the striking stench of piss and some form of shit and garbage all waft by in the soon to be even more baking-hot LA sun. Some folk look quite normal while others are clearly cracked-out and whacked-out. This wasn't what I expected at all. I decide I can't go through with it. *Too dangerous. It's like the village of the damned here. I thought the homeless people on the Hollywood Walk of Fame were bad, but this? Jesus, I'd be lucky if I made it out alive never mind a few dollar-tips and some sausages.* I grab the key inside my backpack to unlock my bike, but before I can say 'Adios' Keanu rocks up in a Hawaiian shirt and flip-flops like he's just come off set of *The OC*.

'You made it, dude – come meet Pappa.'

I didn't realise that 'Pappa', i.e. Keanu's father, would be on the premises today, as from what he's said briefly in the past it's mainly him and his co-workers who run the business (stand) and that his father only oversees things from time to time.

'It's pretty rough around here?!' I say, following behind Keanu, who is now leading me on foot down a side alley as I walk behind him with BMX in tow, still none the wiser what this job entails or more to the point where this mysterious stand is normally set up.

'Nah, it's all good, man. These guys are mainly harmless, as long as you don't get too involved. Just do the business and you get out.'

Slightly flummoxed at his revelation that this is also a hand-delivery hot-dog service and perplexed at how one goes about doing so without being robbed or killed round these parts, I wonder if I've missed something and ask more.

'So, you make the hot dogs on the stand then you . . .?'

Keanu turns round, stopping me in my tracks with a look that implies he's definitely heard enough of my questions.

'DUDE. We are *not* selling hot dogs.'

BA HONOURS

LAX airport, LA, autumn, 2006

One thing I have been having some luck with over the last few years is the odd upgrade on my flights between LA and Manchester. Due to having a couple of pals who are 'trolley dollies', I take it in turns with which one can kindly help bump me up, as it were. All I have to do is buy the ticket at a discount price and they do their thing by putting a word in with the cabin crew. I've even been upgraded before because I was recognised.

Not so much of that of late, though. Maybe I'm too nervous ask anymore, which may have something to do with me feeling like a failure. One of my British Airways pals, Joe – a lovely chap who loves a good gossip – bumped into none other than Louis Walsh on one of his recent flights and took it upon himself to let dear Louis know that he was a friend of 'Kavana's' and that I was 'living in LA working on music and acting', to which

Mr Walsh replied, 'Oh, I know him. He shouldn't bother. He's old-hat now,' making me feel like a failed stand-up comedian from the '80s. My mindset isn't helped by the copious amounts of drugs I take at the Hollywood parties I still get invited to, and the 'He's Kav, a huge pop star in the UK' introduction is now, 'He's Kav, he's from London!' to which they reply, 'Oh, really? Do you know a girl called Rebeccah, she lives in Clapp-hamm?!' to which I reply, 'I'm actually from Manchester!' and then they ask about football, a subject I know very little about.

I have to fly back to deal with family duties and the mounting debt I've been turning a blind eye to. Having been spoiled by flying business class and being slightly on edge over what I have to face at the other end, having to put on the 'All is well in sunny California!' act for the family, I do the unthinkable. When I got my first visa (the one for extraordinary talent and people with a few thousand dollars) I had to put together a catalogue, if you like, of all of my 'successes', a portfolio of magazine covers, newspaper articles, awards and record sales, etc. So I craftily – or desperately, depending on how it's seen (both) – decide to take in my hand luggage the copy of me on the front cover of *Attitude* magazine from five years ago, having decided that this one would appear to be the classiest looking (compared to me with my nipples out on the cover of *Smash Hits*, or posing in a pillow fight with the twins from *Sweet Valley High* on the cover of *Big!*). On this *Attitude* cover I look cool, mysterious, and it says 'Pop's Hot Property: Kavana'. That will do, surely?

It doesn't.

Feeling woozy and a little confident after 2-4-1 Long Island ice teas at LAX, I saunter up to the check-in desk and present the cover of myself and make some excuse about having been booked in economy as an oversight by my 'UK agent' (that doesn't exist) and that due to the time difference 'she' isn't responding to my calls or emails.

'As you can see, I'm really embarrassed to have to do this, oh God! But, er, here I am – look!'

I push the magazine cover across the check-in lady's counter, keeping my index finger over the 'July 1998' date at the top above my Zoolander mush.

'Huh. That's you?!'

'Ayaah yes! It was for my last big UK album campaign!'

(The one that didn't come out.)

'Oh wow! . . . you look a lot older now, sir! Aww, so sweet! But I'm sorry, we don't do upgrades anymore and we are pretty full already. You take care and have a good flight, though!'

I go sit down, defeated, *Attitude* magazine in hand, and decide to give Greg a call. I could do with some of his enthusiasm and zest for life right now. As we chat, I notice a woman with dark glasses boarding the flight. *It can't be. Oh, Jesus, this is embarrassing.* It's only bloody Posh Spice – Victoria Beckham.

'Greg, please keep talking. I need you on the phone until I get to my seat. Bloody Posh Spice is on the same flight. I've not seen her since the Gucci party when they were both dressed in matching leather outfits and she told me off for making fun of David's voice in *Smash Hits* while he was stood there next to her. If she spots me she's bound to see me going towards economy and that will just look tragic. She's going to tell everyone she saw me in beach shorts with a carrier bag and she will know I'm not making it stateside, and I'll never get a chance to make a comeback even in the UK!'

'Dude. Calm the fuck down. Go say hi!'

'Hi?! Jesus no. I can't say "Hi!" like some long-lost pal, are you insane?!'

I go and hide behind a pillar and wait until she gets on. She seems to have disappeared. *Fuck fuck fuck.*

'Last call for London Heathrow, Terminal B,' I hear over the Tannoy.

Jesus. I wish I'd worn my cap. I walk over to the gate, head down with phone glued to ear and pretend to be making a call to someone.

'Right. Yes, sure! OK, cool. Send over the filming dates. Great. Casting director, yes.'

I must be on the phone to my movie agent that no longer exists.

Head down I walk through the tunnel and board the plane. Travellers bustle in line, shoving bags in overhead lockers to the right and being served champagne to the left.

Just as I'm about to take a seat, I hear:

'Hello, you! I thought I recognised that accent. What are you doing on here?'

It's her. She's recognised me, even though I do resemble Huckleberry Finn's long-lost northern brother.

'Oh, I live here! Just heading home for a visit. So good to see you too!'

She didn't say it was good to see me, she asked me what I was doing here.

With that she kisses either side of my cheek and walks into first class.

I see a couple of the air stewards notice our exchange so suddenly feel less embarrassed about the whole check-in desk fiasco, just in case word's got round on one of the walkie-talkies that there's a desperate ex-pop star trying to wheedle his way into an upgrade.

I find my seat in economy, an aisle one with two empties next to me and right by the bog. *Phew. This will do. I wish I'd said more to Victoria. We could have reminisced about doing the Virgin Records summer conference, I could have said I remembered she drank Pimm's and made a joke about my white Kappa tracksuit stage outfit. Not that she'd remember. Oh well. At least she was sweet and forgot about the stupid* Smash Hits *thing.*

Just as I'm about to read the *National Enquirer*, which I've placed inside *GQ* to not too look too trashy, a sweet air hostess kneels down next to me to say something.

'Mr Kavanagh, would you like to get your stuff and follow me please, sir.'

Sir? Stuff?

I grab my carrier bag and backpack and unlock my

seat belt, wondering if I'm about to be arrested or if I'm on the wrong flight.

I follow the kind air hostess up through economy, through club and straight into first class.

'Here you go, sir. Would you like a glass of champagne?'

Not only have I moved to first class but it's the sat directly behind Victoria, who now seems to be snoozing.

'Yes, please. That would be lovely,' I say, feeling like the luckiest remembered famous pop boy on the planet.

I've still no idea to this day if it was down to her requesting for me to be moved up, as she slept most of the journey and we didn't speak again. Whatever it was, though, it made my visit home to face the music that somewhat sweeter.

SUNSET STRIPPED

'Hello, son.'

'Hi, Mum.'

I'm back in LA, stood by the payphone at the Grove farmer's market in Hollywood, using an international phone card I bought for five dollars due to my phone being blocked for not paying the bill on time.

'You must be psychic, I was just thinking about you!'

This is my mum's go-to greeting every time I call, and I always feel sad and a little homesick when I hear her say it.

'Aaaw, well, I was thinking about you too, Mum. That's why I called.'

'Well, that's nice, then. Listen, a letter's come for you, shall I open it?'

I always dread when Mum says this, especially lately as it's usually from an old credit card company or other debts that have been mounting up and that I have turned a blind eye to while out here. I figured as long as I can pay the mortgage on their house and whatever I can throw in towards rent for Greg's attic, then everyone else can get in the queue. I've stopped getting yellow cabs everywhere and use my bicycle instead, and the huge eight-dollar lunch I have at Souplantation's all-you-can-eat soup-and-salad buffet leaves me full all day and night, so the 20 dollars a day I'm now budgeting on is just about manageable.

'Yes, please, Mum. Just open it and read it, if you don't mind. Have you got your glasses?'

We go through this little routine every time a letter comes because the real fact is that Mum likes to open them *before* telling me I've received them. But I have to play dumb while she pretends she doesn't know until the correct amount of paper rustling is made to sound like she's doing it there and then, and I play along with the rigmarole.

'Let's see. Dear Mr Anthony Kavanagh— Oh, hang on, your father's shouting something.'

Mum eventually tells me that a cheque has arrived for £25. Music royalties that I have no idea about. I tell her to keep a hold of it at home as if she takes it to my bank there in her giant handbag it will no doubt get lost or end up covered in bingo marker. I know we need every penny we can get, but I don't want her worrying about £25 . . .

'Hang on, love. Your father's saying he wants to read it to you himself, just to make sure I've got the company right.'

Dad comes on the phone, happy as usual and

sounding great. It's been three years now since the cancer diagnosis and he's never sounded better. *God, I love him so much.* I wish I could tell him that, but hopefully me paying for the house where they both live shows it. After all, 'love is an action not just a word' as Neale Donald Walsch says in the self-help book I'm now helping myself to more than ever.

'Right, son. I think she's got it wrong. Bleedin' 'ell, Rita, will you let me speak to him?!'

'Dear Mr Kavanagh . . .'

Here we go again. I light a cigarette while I wait for Dad to read the same thing as Mum and realise this is his way of saying he loves me too, and that he's keeping an eye on things for me.

'Twenty-five, oh, oh, oh, oh oh.'

'How many 0s are there, Dad?' I say, surprised that even my dad who is usually on the ball is reading it wrong while trying to stay calm in case it's in the hundreds.

Like a miracle sent from not only the heavens above but Jesus, Mary, Joseph and the Wizard of Oz all rolled into one, I find out it's old music royalties somehow backdated and sent to me for £25,000. Thank you, God. Or Taiwan.

'What?!! Now, listen Dad. You MUST keep it safe until Angela and Clint arrive,' I say, while jumping up and down with joy by the phone.

'Oh, don't worry, son. It will go in my top drawer with that special whiskey you bought me for Christmas.' Just as well, seeing as the special M&S festive mini boxset of socks and whiskey no longer contains whiskey after I gulped it down one morning for a much-needed hair of the dog and re-filled it with hot water and PG tips with a promise to replace it.

My sister arriving at theirs tomorrow is perfect timing as they will definitely make sure it goes in the bank safely.

'Thanks, Dad! Ta-ra, then, and ta-ra to Mum.'

'Ta-ra,' Mum echoes in the background.

Wow. Just in the nick of time, right when the chips were down I get saved once again. I take it as a sign that it's happened for a reason, and that it proves that God or the universe or whatever you want to call it is looking out for me. I also believe that God knows that I need my own space again. It's been unbelievably kind of my best friend Greg letting me stay, let's face it, more or less rent-free in the attic, but with him about to head off to Australia to train Brad Pitt while shooting *Troy* for three months it would be weird being there with just his flatmates, agent Daniel and his nice-but-nutty girlfriend Jen. *Maybe I'll sublet somewhere for a while until he gets back. Or better still, maybe it's a good idea to live in a cute little motel for a while on Sunset?*

Spoiler alert – it's not.

My Hollywood, ahem, takeover carries on while basing myself at the Saharan Motel on Sunset Boulevard. My new lodgings will cost a special rate of eighty dollars a night due to me going in for the kill and booking it on a month-to-month basis. Cash. A far cry from the junior suite at the Four Seasons in Beverly Hills I resided in when first arriving in this town, but a true artist must take the rough with the smooth to acquire true grit and insight in this world. My cosy Baghdad Café-inspired daydream of living in a place where other creative strangers will come together and form unique bonds while doing our laundry on site turns more into *The Shining* due to some of the poor-souled clientele looking more like they belong in a mental hospital, including myself by the time I check out. My newfound taste for 'ice' introduced to me by Charles has not only fucked with my mind but my finances too.

I have proven once again that left to my own devices I am a hazard. I must also surrender to the fact that my now six-year dream of making it stateside may not happen. Who am I kidding, it *won't* and never will happen. Robbie Williams I am not, who seems to just live here regardless of fame eluding him, but that's what being a multimillionaire can afford you. My Hollywood candle has well and truly burned out, and not without throwing any last dregs of gasoline on it. I begrudgingly admit defeat and return to the UK to a mountain of debt, complete with a suntan and a dodgy transatlantic accent. No one needs to know it hasn't worked out, though. Instead, and like all good *Smash Hits* award-winning superheroes, I have a plan. A comeback in England is exactly what's needed.

* * *

Four weeks earlier.

I'm still not having sex. Not because I don't want to – I've had the odd post-nightclub snog and fiddle (sounds like my kind of Irish pub) back at the Saharan – but I'm usually too drunk, edgy or coked-up to do anything or, more to the point, rise to the occasion (is there anything worse than feeling paranoid AND horny?). Or I pass out next to whichever suitor has taken up my offer. I've also had a stalker, a British soap actor I met randomly at Club Beige, which takes place every Thursday in a disco-cum-supper club on Hollywood and La Brea. My stalker introduces himself by telling me of his 'work'. Having been here for so long, I had no idea of who he was, which makes a change from the other way round. He's a handsome lad with bizarre but intriguing chat-up lines such as, 'You look rough,' and 'You've not made it yet either, then?' while looking at me like he wants to kill me rather than take me on a date. Normally I'd not put up with such rude behaviour but, vodka goggles on, I'm attracted to him and, like a clichéd gay, am drawn to the fact he's pretending to be 'straight' albeit in the gayest club on the gayest exclusive club night in all of West Hollywood. One insult leads to another and before we know it we're back at my place rolling around the two-twins-pushed-together motel bed on top of its finest polyester bed sheets in a 69 position while trying not to fall through the split.

'You're a dirty little pop flop, aren't you, Kav?' he says, while sucking on me so hard I have to push his head off a few times in order to stop the pain and to provide him with some oxygen. I soon realise that our soap actor is into this kind of 'put down' play, which I think may be some kind of S&M but feels like I'm being bullied into orgasm, which I don't, but he does, climaxing all over me while shouting 'Jeeeeeeeesuuuuuuuus.'

The next morning, I wake up, or come to rather, to see him pacing up and down cursing on the phone to his agent about the job he hasn't booked.

'But they fuckin' LOVED me! They really LOVED me!'

I admire his self-delusion, having been there myself, but I need him out, and pronto.

'You'll call me later, yes? Don't forget?'

'Sure,' I reply, in full people-pleasing mode while hoping to never see the nutter again.

From that moment, I can't shake Mr Soap off. He turns up to the motel unannounced so I have to hide in the toilet. He appears lurking outside the gym where I have to tell him I have an important meeting to go to, and on one occasion he leaves 12 voicemails in a row declaring his undying love/hate for me depending on which one you listen to.

I *do* have to get in touch with him, though, when I start to ooze white cream out of the eye of my penis with a ferocious itch to go along with it. Since he was the only person I'd had sex with in a while, I ask him if he has had any issues down there, to which he lovingly replies, 'No, you idiot,' but after sheepishly going to the gay men's walk-in sexual health clinic I find out that I have in fact got the clap. Needless to say, I stop answering his calls, texts and messages and he eventually gets the point. He does leave one final farewell text that simply said, 'Stop Ignoring me U FagGut' [sic].

Who said romance was dead?

MURDER ON THE PANEL FLOOR

London, 2007

I am in the passenger seat of a blacked-out Mercedes being driven through London, randomly thinking about the time a serious-faced Bono looked me deep in the eyes and said, 'Whatever you do, Kavanagh, don't do coke.' It was the late nineties and we were in the VIP area of Browns nightclub surrounded by supermodels and London's fashion elite, after I had somehow found myself inside chatting to the Irish rock star who no doubt felt a bit sorry for me being there by myself and took it upon himself to tell me to steer clear of the devil's drug at all times. I've still to this day got no idea why he said it at that moment, as it hadn't been discussed prior nor was he partaking, but my God do I wish I'd listened.

What started out as 'drinks and food' at a new

swanky place called Somerset House, which I assumed was in Devon and a bit of a way to go for a night out, ends up with me being back at a debauched house party in Notting Hill playing charades with a woman wearing her dead mother's wedding dress and not getting to bed until 5am. To add insult to injury, I am due on TV at 12:30pm today on a show called *Loose Women* to promote my *Best of Kavana* album – a stretch of a title but better than *Greatest Hits*, unless you're from Taiwan – which has been curated by a knowledgeable and kind fan free of charge and flung out by Virgin Records to no doubt recoup some of my label debt after noticing my profile rise due to my recent stint on a Saturday night talent show called *Grease Is the Word* where I came second (after being told by the producer I'd won by a 'shoe-in' with the public all week, but mysteriously lost on the night). I was secretly drinking throughout filming, which I thought I'd got away with. It was probably for the best as the prize, which was a year-long stint playing Danny Zuko in London's West End, would have been a bit tricky while slurping vodka in the wings before going on to lead the company in a hand jive. Having entered the competition – after being told by various music managers I had no chance making a comeback without getting on such a reality show – I have now found myself being 'famous' again after the best part of a lost decade in LA and yet I still seem to be oblivious to when to call it a night before a work day.

The fear and dread are all-consuming the next morning (or should I say, three hours later) as we bump along the motorway to arrive at ITV studios. I'm not sure I can go through it, and if I must, I may have no choice but to down a giant hair of the dog to stop the quaking and panic before we arrive.

'Excuse me, is there any way we could stop at a shop please?' I whimper to the driver, who has Starship's 'Nothing's Gonna Stop Us Now' on Smooth FM blaring on his front speakers only, a fitting tribute to my almighty craving and desperation to get my hands on some alcohol ASAP.

'Sorry, sir, no stopping as traffic is bad.'

This is not good. I am in an almighty hell of my own doing and there is no way on God's mighty earth I can enter that building without a drink.

'I'm sorry, I must stop, I need some snacks for my blood sugar.' I've no idea what I mean by this feeble excuse, and judging his expression in the rearview mirror nor does he. There's already a complimentary bottle of water, a carton of orange juice, some mini salted pretzels and *The Times* on the seat next to me. What more does a bloodshot-eyed, paranoid wreck of a human need?

'OK, there is something coming up. You must be quick.'

Once he parks up on the side of the road with the engine running, I hotfoot it into the Nisa Express like a bedraggled dying wench and purchase two half-litre bottles of vodka, shoving one into each of my suit jacket pockets. The square bottles fit perfectly in each. It's the same suit jacket I was wearing last night, which is luckily black along with the now-crumpled stale cigarette/Febreze-stenched shirt I'm also wearing after not making it back to my hotel.

I jump in the car and off we drive with me taking no prisoners and polishing off a quarter of one of the bottles in one go. Within seconds, me and my 'blood sugar' are all back to being somewhat robust and I sink back into the cream leather car seat, finally relaxing. *Whatever I do, I must not have too much and get drunk.* I'll pace myself. Even though the recording isn't for another two hours. Thank God they insisted on me lip-syncing the vocals as I've all the vocal stamina of Kermit the Frog.

Once in my dressing room I plonk into a chair and stare at my reflection. I look puffy and greasy having had no time to shower, instead going for what my mother calls a 'swill', which although could sound like something you would give animals in a farmyard is actually quite handy when you're in a rush in a stranger's bathroom. I've also now got the hiccups so go in search of the green room. Alcohol to me is like liquid energy that lights me up, not calms me down. I need to keep moving rather than sit. I see other people happily sip their wine slowly or take their time over a cocktail and I just don't get it. All this, 'a drink helps me wind down after a busy day' is alien to me. I've also noticed this chemical change happen since I returned from America, weird, like some kind of progression – it's like my body now craves it, and once I have a drink it seems there is no mental or physical defence to not have another, an all-consuming need for more.

While deciding what soft drink I will choose from the green room (i.e. which one will look less suspect once I pour vodka into it) one of the production staff asks me if I'm OK? To which, in my paranoia, I say of course and perfectly wonderful by myself thank you. I think it's best I go back to the dressing room and pace around there rather than here.

With vodka now hitting all the right confidence-inducing spots for my big TV comeback, I notice one of the hosts, and all-round icon, Jane McDonald's dressing-room door open.

'Hi, Jane, I'm KAV!' I announce loudly, holding in my stomach which is more or less impossible while trying not to hiccup, standing in her doorway while she gazes back.

'Oh, 'ello, cock. How are you?'

The connection is instant. I can feel it. The warmth of the stare, the possible wink of the eye (although I am starting to see double).

'I'm on the show today, you know! I hope you'll all be nice to me!' I exclaim like a spoilt Dickensian child, hoping my soon-to-be-best-pal Jane has a word with the other panellists to go easy as it's common knowledge they can be brutal, especially Carol McGiffin who doesn't seem to take any prisoners.

'Oh, you'll be fine, cocker. It's camp as tits out there.'

A huge wave of Jane and Smirnoff relief washes over me. If my new northern soulmate tells me it will be fine, it will be.

'Ta-ra, then – see you out there!' I say, hamming up

my accent a little more to match Jane's and to let her know I also feel the deep, deep bond we now have and will forever more. A new sister, perhaps? I envision ourselves walking Blackpool prom with chip butties after her sell-out show at the Opera House followed by a raucous night just the two of us at Funny Girls drag club in the VIP bar before heading back to her glamorous seaside palace and talking showbiz. I could do my Les Dawson impressions, and as the dawn comes in she will serenade me with 'You're My World' before we fall into a deep slumber in matching best-friend silk pyjamas.

* * *

'Hi, Kav. Can you call me back, please? It's urgent.'

The following morning I am once again hungover and having my well-needed hair of the dog. Only this time I'm drinking cans of beer, in a single bed, in a bedsit-cum-hotel in Paddington.

My phone battery went dead at some point yesterday afternoon, having had no charger or the noggin to ask to borrow one and, due to the amount I drank, also forgot to buy one. I did however at some point after my TV filming somehow manage to get halfway across the city and book myself into this quaint establishment along with buying a late-night feast of what looks like an empty kebab tray, a pizza box and the remains of a Cadbury Creme Egg.

I can't remember much of my 'performance' on *Loose Women* yesterday apart from the odd flashback, which every time one comes I slug another mouthful of beer at the harrowing thought. When someone, especially your new TV and theatre agent, leaves you a voicemail at 10am saying it's urgent it's usually not the best news, is it?

'It's not good.'

Gulp.

'I'm afraid they're not happy with you at ITV. They have given you a lifetime ban on *Loose Women*. You can never go on again.'

Jesus.

My weary agent goes on to tell me what happened. It's rough when you hear from a friend about your drunken antics from the night before, let alone what happened on *national television* or, worse, what happened behind the scenes of the show, which I remember none of. What doesn't help matters is that this is the same agent who only a month ago, and after a very promising first audition and callback for the role of Che in the regional tour of *Evita*, had to make excuses for me as to why I turned up to the last and most important callback slaughtered at 1pm, not knowing any of my lines or the words to 'Oh What a Circus', instead insisting on singing Eva Perón's 'Don't Cry for Me Argentina'. Horrific.

'Well, firstly, you scarpered,' says the new posh agent, with me having no idea what such a word means. He goes on.

'You went missing for 15 minutes before you were due on air, you had a whole studio of workers running around after you, and were found in the pub opposite with minutes to go.'

'Oh, er, I'm sorry,' I say, feeling like a naughty schoolboy in the headmaster's office except I'm now a 32-year-old man drinking beer in bed on a Wednesday morning.

'You asked Carol McGiffin live on air when was the last time she had sex, and you were described as being loud and unhinged backstage by the producer, asking for wine and demanding everyone join you in the pub after the show.'

He continues.

'You then had to be escorted off the premises and helped into the car by the driver, who by the way nearly didn't agree to take you, due to you being so drunk.'

Oh.

'You then insisted he reroute the booking and take you all the way to Soho and drop you there.'

That would explain the poppers next to the kebab box, then.

'I'm afraid we as an agency need to have a think about where we go from here, but in the meantime please sort yourself out.'

With that the phone is put down, along with me feeling like I should be too. I extend the room for another night, and head over to the cosy pub across the street. Those cans of beer aren't quite cutting it.

DINNER FOR SIX

Faye Dunaway keeps calling me Kevin. I know for a fact that Prince Azim of Brunei, whose London palace we are about to have dinner at, introduced me as 'Kavana', but Faye clearly misheard it and I haven't had the guts to correct her as yet. I got the call late afternoon from Prince Azim inviting me to dinner tonight, and after a quick dash back to my Kentish Town bedsit and change of attire I made my way here, luckily with just enough tube fare on my Oyster card to do so. I haven't seen Azim since his birthday party a couple of years ago when Diana Ross sang one song with a wind machine on the dance floor, and I attempted to flirt with a handsome millionaire called Ivan. The time before that was my all-expenses paid trip to Brunei with Greg, so to say times have changed a little would be an understatement. I think in the prince's eyes I'm still nineties pop star Kavana, untouched by the cruel realities of life, but I haven't told him any different.

It's not like I can just call him up and say, 'Hey, Prince, did I tell you my career is in the bin and I have no real place to live? Oh and guess what? I think I have a drink problem! Wanna hang out?'

Anyway, the other guest at this lovely dinner for six is the one and only Jerry Hall who, like me, is wondering if there's a suitable area one can go for a cigarette because that's exactly what she said in her gorgeous Texan drawl.

'Where do we go for a smoke around here, y'all?' to be exact, to which one of the waiting kitchen staff escorts us out into the courtyard.

I was worried that, Brunei being a dry country, Prince Azim's soiree tonight may follow suit, so I'd prepared. But the mini Tesco Chardonnay I'd downed on the way is now sadly wearing off.

Faye has brought along her son and his fiance. Her son is a handsome American jock who is also her manager and one of the reasons the Oscar-winning legendary Hollywood actress is here. Her and Azim are going into business together, the prince acting as producer/funder for her labour-of-love passion project, which is making a movie biopic of Maria Callas with Ms Dunaway playing the lead. This, according to Azim on a private chat/gossip on the phone with me, is becoming a tricky issue for the project given Faye's age, but Faye gets what Faye wants, which currently is some weighing scales to weigh the food we are about to eat. It doesn't appear that Jerry and Faye are the best of friends judging by the awkward silences at the dinner table, but for me it's just another night in my random life of having one foot in being a pop star and the other hoping I make the last tube home and hopefully the McDonald's saver menu while I'm at it.

AMY

Sunday afternoon, Camden, 2008

I'm sitting in the pub post a Sunday lunch gathering with some old pals from the TV and music world. I skipped the actual eating part due to being low on funds. I've been back on the London scene for a bit now and am living above a pub in Kentish Town for £150 a week cash. It's a tiny little room but it's handy to get to and from appointments or studio sessions I grab when I can depending on who wants to work with me, which is slim pickings since I've ventured into the reality world. Some old friends of mine who are doing well as writers for other artists aren't keen on working with me, even though in the past they have told me what a talented songwriter I am. The word is being spread that I'm on the lookout for my own record deal, not as a songwriter for hire, regardless of my talent, and no one wants to be attached to a drunken former pop star on the comeback trail. Word of my erratic behaviour is everywhere. What am I supposed to do? The reality show *Grease Is the Word* was really my only option, but now no one is taking me seriously. Or at least that's what I'm telling myself the reason is, when deep down I know it has a lot more to do with my drinking and unreliability.

Sitting alone, slurping my third Guinness on this wet Sunday afternoon after my friends all moved on to Soho House (I passed on their suggestion of joining as the cab split alone will leave me scrimping and scraping, never mind the cost of an overpriced gin and tonic), I spot two girls looking over and talking at the bar. I'm sure I recognise one of them, but instead pretend to look at my all-important messages (of which there are none). My predictions seem to be confirmed when I go over to the bar and, now with a good amount of Irish courage in me, say hello. It's mainly for a bit of company more than anything but I'm also out of cigarettes, and I've seen one of them pop out to the smoking area a few times, gabbing away on her phone as she does it.

'Hi, it's Kav, right? I'm a friend of Amy's,' she says, smiling.

Amy? Amy who? She's got the first bit right with my name, but I can't think of who she means. The amount of people I've met over the years it could be anyone.

'Oh, right,' I say. 'Which Amy?'

'Amy Winehouse,' she says. 'She's our mate. I'm Catriona and this is Chan.'

'Oh, that Amy!' I respond, suddenly remembering I have met *that* Amy a few years ago at the 19

Management Christmas party where we got chatting in the lift. I think I vomited next to an extremely lovely Annie Lennox and I ended up with Amy and her pals in an R&B club where she gave me water before telling me to get my arse in a taxi home. She was definitely a force to be reckoned with and a caring one at that.

'She's at home now and said to come back with us. She loves you!'

Blimey. This Amy – the one who loves me and is obviously going to be my new best friend – wants to invite me back to her flat in Camden? This Amy who is a huge star and has been nominated for a Grammy wants to see me?!

I take up their offer and head over to meet her. *If I'd known this would happen I might have put something a bit cooler on, this floral-printed shirt and jeans from Primark is fine for a pub (liquid) lunch but not what I'd have chosen to wear to meet someone as cool as Amy.*

I wonder if she has a beehive all the time? I wonder if she's as wild as they say in the papers? I have to admit that I also wonder if her and her mates have any drugs. Guinness makes you sleepy, I need perking up a bit.

The fresh air, Guinness and wine hit me just as we arrive at Amy's flat in Camden. A tidy little place it seems and not some derelict drug-and-booze-ridden squat you'd imagine by the way she's described in the press. A few cool-looking types are sat around playing music, the atmosphere is super mellow and not what I had in mind or expected. *So much for a wild party.*

I take it upon myself to head to the kitchen and see a woman tiptoeing over the stove in ballet bumps. *It's her.*

"Ello, stranger. How are you?!' she says with all the welcome of the Artful Dodger to my Oliver Twist. She reaches in for a hug over the stove, her tiny frame round mine. I'm not great with hugs, but it feels genuine with her, like she means it.

'I'm good, thanks,' I lie, wondering if she really is alcohol-dependant like me and in the hope she will offer me a drink now I'm at my 'feeling flat and craving more' anxious level and in desperate need of topping up.

'Who've you come dressed as? Alfie Moon?'

I knew the shirt was a mistake, but I like the icebreaker and suddenly feel relaxed for a few seconds, some grace under my bodily cravings for more booze.

'You help yourself to whatever you want, my darling. Oh, my God, look at your eyelashes, you'd make a beautiful girl, wouldn't ya?!'

Phew. I grab a glass and pour some red wine from off the counter into it and knock it back in one, keeping my back to her so she doesn't see and in the hope I can down another one before she notices.

'Easy, you'll be pissed.' Of course she noticed, us types get each other. 'You want some meatballs, then?'

'Er, yes please, that would be lovely.'

The thought of eating makes me feel a bit sick, but I can't be rude. I hope she's not trying to do the trick my sister does either, all that 'eating soaks up the booze' crap. Yes, it does indeed soak up the booze, but it also makes you flat as a pancake and want to go to bed straight after as far as I'm concerned.

'Go on, then. Get a plate,' she says, pointing over to the sink where they are, and I grab one.

'Now go sit yourself down and get it down ya.'

'OK,' I say, and like a good boy walk into the other room, even though I'd much rather stay with her in the kitchen.

'Oi,' she says as I'm halfway out the door.

I turn round and see a silhouette of a beehive holding a spoon against the late-afternoon Camden sun. A perfect picture.

'Bon appétit, CHAVANA, hahahahahahaha!'

And with that an unusual and genuine friendship is born, one which will be much more profound to me later on in life, but for now I leave, with a piping-hot plate of her home-made meatballs in hand to the sound of her cackles down the hallway. It's a laugh that will echo in my mind and visit me in my dreams when I need it the most.

I TOLD YOU I WAS TROUBLE

'**M**r Kavanagh, there is a Ms Winehouse for you at the stage door.'

The slightly jobsworth woman announces this through the intercom in my dressing room where I have currently been residing while playing Prince Charming at the Milton Keynes Theatre. 'If my friends could see me now!' as it's sung in *Sweet Charity*, well, they have, only this friend has come to witness me in *Cinderella* alongside Bobby Davro as Buttons and Anthea Turner as the Fairy Godmother. I did tell Amy on the phone this morning, after she declared 'I've never seen a panto in my life', that it wasn't exactly Shakespeare and was she sure she wanted to make such a trip to the bright lights of Milton Keynes where I am staying in a Travelodge for the run after the heating pipe burst in the theatre digs I was renting, but she insisted and here we are.

My role as the Prince is one of the few jobs I've booked the whole year. It came about after a call from an agent I had a meeting with while in a semi-wine-induced blackout in her office in Soho – I'd spent the afternoon pre-meeting mustering up some pizazz, culminating in me getting pissed, but somehow got through it. She said, rather than take me on, she would keep an eye out for stuff in the future, which I at the time read as a polite way of saying 'not for us'. But here we are. The main 'star' of the show and her actual client, Ben Adams, lead singer of pop group A1, originally booked the role but then had other commitments in Norway (where his band are still huge, apparently) for the first two weeks of the panto run. It beggars belief why he took the role in the first place, only being able to be the part-time Prince, but one must not complain as Mr Adams' pop commitments in the land of the Vikings have given yours truly a four-week booking (including rehearsals) and £2.5k just in time for Christmas. It's a little disheartening seeing Ben's face on the posters outside the Milton Keynes Theatre, but a job is a job after all.

Word has also now got round the building that superstar Amy Winehouse is here, so as I make my way to the stage door I am harassed by the same villagers from the ensemble and one of the ugly sisters who fell out with me last week for, well, let's just say my slightly merry matinee performance after one too many medicinal ports to 'help with vocals' (hair of the dog) who is now suddenly my best friend.

'Oh, please let us meet her.'

'Oh, I adore her.'

Yadda yadda . . .

I arrive at the stage door to find Amy in a full-length winter coat with beehive on point and her friend/right-hand man Tyler, who judging by his face is aware we could be in for a bumpy night, as Amy has also brought three girls she has just met at the Milton Keynes KFC en route and invited them as a kind gesture. After I give Amy a huge hug and say hi to the others, I escort them through to my dressing room where I am mid getting dressed as the Prince in golden long johns, buckled shoes and tights, with enough panto make-up on to give Christopher Biggins a run for his money.

'Oh. My. God,' says Amy. 'You look *beautiful*, Chav,' which by now is her new pet name for me. She congratulates me on my gawdy palette and Blackadder get-up.

'Where's Cinderella, then?'

I try to explain to Amy that it's nearly showtime and the kind usher will be escorting her and her friends to their seats, which unbeknown to me are three rows from the front and completely in my eyeline. Next door to me in her dressing room is Anthea Turner who has been a bloody good support to me on this run, having seen I may not be doing great in my personal life and being one of the few not to scold me on my matinee disaster.

'Oh, hello!' says Amy, after having spotted sweet Anthea who is now in full Fairy Godmother attire, holding her magic wand and due to go on for the opening of act one.

'Oh, hello there. Lovely to meet you, darling.'

Anthea can see the hullabaloo that's happening outside our dressing rooms with even the wardrobe assistants now casually happening to walk by to watch the circus that's in full swing backstage, never mind on it.

'Why don't we go in my dressing room?'

I am now standing in my dressing room with Amy and Anthea, dressed as the Fairy Godmother to my now slightly nervous prince, wondering if Amy, who seems to have had a few already (and who can blame her on a drive to Milton Keynes?), is going to be able to behave herself during the performance, the audience to which consists of parents and children and her pals from KFC who don't seem to be the quietest of theatregoers either.

'Oi, Anthea,' says Amy. 'I loved you on *Blue Peter*. Have you got any sticky-back plastic?'

What she really means is a plaster due to the graze Amy has somehow got her on arm, and in true Fairy Godmother style Anthea comes to the rescue with some sticky tape and a baby wipe.

'Aww, thank you, Fairy Anthea. You're beautiful, you are,' says Amy. And with that she gives me a big hug and her and her entourage are taken to their seats while I pray to God it'll be alright on the night.

My entrance as the posh prince doesn't happen until we get through half of act one and right after the first introduction of the ugly sisters, where they and Cinderella are due to sing their big first number.

'OIIIIII!! LEAVE CINDERELLA ALONE, YOU BITCHES!'

Jesus.

It's Amy who I can hear screaming at the top of her lungs from the audience in defence of poor Cinderella.

'OOOOI, YOU TWO UGLY SISTERS ARE BITCHES!!!'

She's not giving up. Fuck. I can hear the audience start to chatter among themselves and children either crying or asking Mummy who that strange woman is shouting in the audience.

I somehow get through my entrance number of Take That's 'Shine', which I have to sing to a puzzled Dandini while Amy wolf-whistles throughout.

'THERE'S MY PRINCE CHARMING, WIT WOOOO!'

At least she's enjoying herself and I do feel a sense of flattery singing such a song dressed as a posh imbecile in white tights and 18th-century shoes.

As I come off at the end of act one and the interval there's chaos backstage. The ugly sisters in particular, who were Amy's biggest fans before the show, are now demanding to 'GET HER OUT OF HERE! SHE IS RUINING THIS PERFORMANCE!'

Amy and her pals are brought backstage during the interval and she apologises for getting carried away, which at this point I'm starting to find quite funny. Thank Christ it's my last night before the main prince takes over. I've done enough walks of shame on this bloody show, I don't think I could handle another scolding from the company manager in the morning.

'I'M SO SORRY, CHAV. I GET OVEREXCITE-ABLE. I PROMISE TO BE QUIET IN THE NEXT BIT.'

'OK, Amy, it's fine. Just be mindful of the other people, I love it but we have to be careful, OK?'

It's decided that Amy and crew will be put in the upper dress circle for the second half of the show and everything seems to be going fine until my big entrance number of Frankie Goes To Hollywood's 'The Power of Love', which I have to sing in one dramatic spotlight holding Cinderella's lost silver slipper. As I reach for the high note in the chorus while positioning the slipper up in the air and singing to it, I hear:

'GO ON, CHAV!!! I LOVE YOU, PRINCE CHARRRRRMIN, WIT WOO WOOOHOOO-HOOOOO!'

Then out of nowhere there is the sound of what can only be described as two hyenas fighting from the balcony and then complete silence. For the rest of the show neither I nor any of my beloved ensemble know what's happened.

We find out after the show that after being told by a rather heavy-handed usher twice the size of Amy that she must be quiet or leave, Amy whacked him one and was removed from the building with the police called. I get a call the next day from her apologising profusely, not that she needs to, having done worse myself, inviting me over once again for her home-made meatballs. That night we drink vodka and she plays the drums while I play the keyboards.

'I'm so sorry if I got you in trouble, Chav.'

'Don't you worry, we've all been there. Plus them ugly sisters *were* bitches to Cinderella.' We fall asleep next to each other and I wake up early the next day on Christmas Eve and see it's snowing. I leave my friend to sleep while I head back up north for what will, unbeknown to me, be our last Christmas with my father.

POTTERS

A shopping trolley. A bloody shopping trolley. Due to the fact I haven't owned a suitcase in years and my budget is low, I had to purchase said trolley to carry all my worldly wares on the next outgoing train to Great Yarmouth from Liverpool Street station, where I'm about to start my new job. My old gig agent and friend Sue has somehow convinced me this is a good idea, and quite frankly I'm all out of ideas myself. Sue lives there and knows the entertainments manager of the 'only six-star holiday park in the UK – Potters', and has negotiated a three-month contract with them where I will perform as 'nineties pop sensation Kavana' (me apparently) after the main cabaret show for the season. 'Kavana' and 'cabaret' were not supposed to go in the same sentence, but I will turn yet another blind eye to my somewhat flailing career for now. I will be paid £350 a week *and* I will get my own free accommodation. This works highly in my favour as not only have I burned every 'room at the inn' bridge offered by my friends since moving back from LA, but I am skint. All gig offers have dried up and my TV and theatre agent has fired me, after the last audition he sent me on was a disaster, thanks to me overindulging the night before and thinking three large Chardonnays at Wetherspoons to calm the nerves pre-audition was a good idea – it wasn't.

Part of me thinks this new job could be the perfect tonic for my depression – a reset, if you like. I get my own digs, I'll be by the sea and I get to sing in front of an already-booked audience every night – and do it all under the radar. No one needs to know outside of the cosy six-star resort on ye olde Great Yarmouth's land.

The other seven parts of me are worried sick I will hate it and 'pop sensation Kavana' will be the laughing stock of the holiday park. I also have an inkling Potters may just want a little more from me than first said. The words 'entertainment team' was mentioned (*gulp*) and that they may require me to 'help out' on the odd day. Out of fear, I haven't actually checked what this means and, even though Sue has sheepishly assured me, 'It will be fine, love. They want YOU. You're a big booking!' I can't help envisioning myself as some kind of out-of-his-depth redcoat teaching the 'Cha-Cha Slide' to a gaggle of overenthusiastic holidaymakers from Clacton.

I find a seat in the train carriage and pull out my new hardback diary I bought yesterday in the pound shop. I skip to tomorrow, 1st May, and begin to write a list.

Lists are good. Lists mean you have your shit together. *I am good and I have my shit together.*

MONDAY 1ST MAY
  *Wake up 9am
  *Take antidepressant (double to help with first-day nerves)
  *Beach run for 20 mins
  *Light breakfast from resident buffet (bring to chalet and eat in private)
  *Go over set list and make a decision re: Lionel Richie cover – remember it's a crowd-pleaser
  *Use on-site gym
  *Buy wine (for AFTER gig not before)
  *Rehearse
  *Showtime!

Feeling cautiously proud of having a new routine in place, I treat myself to a Ginsters pork and apple slice and a decaf coffee at the on-board buffet bar. I am literally becoming more Alan Partridge by the minute, not to mention I have to change at Norwich. Maybe I'll do some community radio while I'm there just to really top it off. *Jesus. All I need now is to find out there's a Corby trouser press in the room, with a welcome pack of shortbread fingers and an unlimited supply of Nescafé Gold Blend. Was I really on* Top of the Pops *once?*

YOUR FATHER

January, 2010

The call I've been dreading arrives. While sitting on the toilet in a three-bedroomed caravan in Clacton on Sea. My dad is dying and, judging by my brother-in-law's gentle but serious tone on the phone, it's going to be sooner rather than later.

'Hi, Anthony. I hope you're OK? I think you might want to think about coming back, you know, today or tonight?'

Clint has always been the more sensible and calmer one in these situations. My sister and I are too emotional and hate confrontation at the best of times, and with Mum's early signs of what we think is dementia, bless her, she is in no fit state to deliver news like this.

'But I'm in Clacton, Clint, after the holiday park gig last night!'

I say 'gig' but last night's was more me performing to an audience of sunburned holidaymakers who talked throughout while keeping an eye on their buggies and their kids who were sat cross-legged on the dance floor in front of me after an exhausted redcoat led the 'Macarena' and I slurped a pint of wine masquerading as lime and soda to help with my nerves.

'But I thought they were going to try him with more food. It's not cancer anyway, he's just stopped eating.'

'It's time, Anthony. Just come back.'

There's no rehearsal for getting a call like this the one you've been dreading since you were a child. No one ever tells you how to act or feel, it's just something that happens. I don't know what's worse, though, being told someone you adore, who told you clouds were made of marshmallows that you floated on when you were sleeping and was able to remove his whole thumb and magically put it back on over and over, was dead or that he was dying. For me it's the latter and means having to wait and endure the pain and denial of what's ahead but to have to do it sober because you've got a five-hour train journey ahead to Manchester and need to keep your wits about you to deal with the absolute hell you've got to face as well as be the supportive son and brother when you get there. Just as well they paid me the £350 in cash last night otherwise I'd be asking poor Clint for the train fare too.

I don't even bother cleaning up the caravan wine bottle and fast food mess I made post my performance before the main Tina Turner tribute act last night, who sounded more like Rod Stewart. It worked a treat in 'It Takes Two' but not so much in 'Private Dancer', especially when he went into the crowd, some of which were mardy toddlers wanting bed not an athletic foghorn in a red leather miniskirt and wig gyrating by the leftover cold chicken meal deals. I sometimes wonder if my life could be any more bizarre, and why the cosmos or God has dealt me this card or cards of late? What is the test in all this? I drink the last of the now cold coffee and barter with myself whether to take the last diazepam I got from the doctor for 'anxiety' where I lied about how many units of alcohol I drink and how it's definitely playing a part in me waking up feeling like I've got an elephant sat on my chest, regardless of the other factors that add to it. It should get me through the journey at least. I'll deal with my no doubt desperately sad waiting audience when I get to the hospital.

The journey is long and I spend most of it staring out the window, partly to not show my tears, which are finally being released after holding them in for way too long, and partly to avoid the snacks and drinks trolley with mini white and red wines and miniature spirits teasing me out of the corner of my eye. I know just a couple would immediately take the edge of my sadness and shock, but also begin the all-consuming craving that would get lit in this cursed chemical make-up I've been given and not allow me to stop.

The hospital ward is bright. I search for my family, mainly looking for Mum's wheelchair sticking out by the bed as it usually does, having been in one for a while now while we wait for her hip operation she's been putting off, much to Dad's worry and exhaustion, having always been the more domesticated of the two. I sometimes wonder if me losing the house along with Mum's early dementia and her inability to get around ran him into the ground and he's had enough. Literally. What with that and witnessing a son whose life is clearly on a downward spiral – something obvious to all but me – I can't really blame him wanting some respite. I just didn't expect it to come to this. I first spot my sister, Angela. My beautiful sister. We are more alike than we care to admit, which in one way makes us best friends but in other ways not say what needs to be said. Love is an action, though; I have seen more proof of that with her patience and putting up with my erratic behaviours recently to know that.

'Oh, here he is. Have you just come off the stage?'

Mum sits at the end of the bed chewing one of Dad's Cadbury Roses chocolates that he's not touched.

'Yes, Mum. Just got off the train now!' I reply, not wanting to correct her seeing as it is half true. It just wasn't the West End as she likes to tell everyone regardless.

I hug Angela and Clint, the three of us knowing things are not good but keeping up the act of pretending it's all normal for Mum's sake. Just another night at the hospital, the one he's been in for six months and now is never coming home from. Dad is in the bed, in and out of sleep like a skin-covered skeleton. His tattoo that says 'Rita' on his left arm, that I used to colour in with felt-tip pens when I was little, seems to have gone from faded green to grey, his face gaunt and hollow with only his dark eyelashes and shamrock-green eyes looking the same.

'Hello, Dad. I've come to see you. You OK?' I smile and pick up his lukewarm hand and hold it while Mum rustles chocolate wrappers, oblivious behind me, and Angela and Clint take a well-earned five-minute walk up the ward.

My dad opens his eyes and looks right into mine.

'Son . . . Aren't you lonely?' he says quietly, before closing his eyes for one of the last times . . . It seems even in his exhausted, morphine-induced state my father knows me much better than I ever thought he did.

* * *

The next few days are a blur. Mum's two sisters (my aunties) who also work at the hospital and were his guardian angels during his illness, sitting with him and taking it turns bringing him home-cooked food, do the same with me and Mum now it's just the two of us. We're no longer living in the hope of Dad's return, it's now funeral arrangements and viewing his body at the funeral home, which I can't bear to do. So instead I sit in the outside waiting room and hear my mother's wails when she sees the man she married 50 years ago in a coffin in his favourite shirt. I never want to see the dead body of someone I love. Ever.

I make a fool of myself at the wake after drinking straight vodka to get me through the funeral part, apparently standing on a garden chair in the yard melodramatically weeping and shouting 'where is Daddy?' (something I hadn't called him since I was approximately five years old). Once again allowing alcohol to take centre stage quite literally and not even allow myself the dignity to show some respect.

It seems 'Daddy' was somewhere, though, as the day after the funeral I am home alone. Angela and Clint are on 'Mum duty', taking her to the market in some hope of maintaining some bit of normality in the absolute shitshow of grief and sadness, and I go into my newly allocated single bedroom back at Mum's after the move and sit on the mattress I couldn't be bothered getting a bed frame for. I lie down on the bed and stare at the ceiling and say:

'Dad, if you are there, anywhere, PLEASE give me a sign.'

I wait . . . and wait . . . and nothing. I decide to go all out so roll onto the carpet and get on my knees and ask again:

'DAD, PLEASE, PLEASE, GIVE ME A SIGN!'

More tears come and I put my head onto the floor sobbing. It all comes out, every last drop I've been holding in for as long as I can remember. Not just grief for my father, but for my mother's loss of her husband, for my sister's loss, for the loss of the house and their security which could have started all this, the loss of my so-called fucking career, the loss of money, hope, loss of every single relationship I managed to screw up because alcohol came first, loss of dignity, self-respect, real joy I haven't felt in years without having to put a drink inside me first to be able to feel just a moment's relief from a mind that either wants me in a nuthouse or dead.

Loss of myself.

I wipe my tears with the unwashed duvet on the bed on the floor next to me and pull myself up. They will be back from taking Mum shopping soon, and the last thing they need to see is me in a state like this.

The thought randomly occurs to me to go over to the pile of books on the floor, including one in a Waterstones bag I hid underneath all the others that I bought for Dad to read in hospital. I never got to take it to him. My dad loved going to the cinema by himself and not long before he got sick he came back one day and went on and on about this film *Looking For Eric*, something do with a football fan and Eric Cantona, which Ken Loach directed. With him being an avid reader too, I bought him the book. I take it out of the bag and another wave of tears comes. He would have loved reading this. I can see him sat up in his bed with his glasses on smiling:

'Bleedin' 'ell! That's great that, Antney,' he'd say in his half-Manc, half-Dublin accent. You could wrap up a 10-pence coin in newspaper and he'd act like you'd given him a diamond, my dad.

My dad.

I grab the book and take it with me into the toilet for a read. Anything to take my mind off what's happening. I open it on a random page, which is totally blank except for the name of the chapter, which is two words:

Your Father.

There's also a brand-new £20 note tucked into the

spine. Considering my father never made it home since I bought the book, and my mother now can't walk up the stairs, there is no way anyone could have put it in there. I take it as the sign I asked for.

I go to the off-licence and buy a bottle of wine, a half-bottle of vodka and some cigarettes. My dad knows I need it more than ever right now.

THE FAITHFUL

'That's right, you are a good little katty,' says Frida, my new friend, who is also a fan, who has been one of the very kind 'rooms at the inn', shall we say, upon my visits back and forth to London over the last year or so. I'm still pursuing my dream of getting back out there again after my confidence-boosting, but at times terrifying, holiday-park experience. Frida, my new and faithful friend, another one in a longish line of people who invite me into their homes to 'stay a few days', which somehow turns into weeks or even months depending on how much of a loose cannon I am (and also depending if they like a drink or three). Either way, it usually goes tits-up for reasons such as them discovering I've drunk their expensive vodka (any type would have done) and refilled it with water, or rocked up keyless, banging on the window one too many times after an all-nighter at some random's house.

I do, however, have a new agent – a charming man

who likes a drink also, which is convenient for me as my now nearing-two bottles-of-wine-a-day habit (only after 5pm, though) won't pay for itself and I am more or less skint. I have booked a job playing a knight! Yes, as in 'of the round table' knight. I shall be doing a fringe play, which I was told by my new agent over a bottle of Chablis at Balans in Soho, is London's answer to 'off Broadway' and it's quite common for a fringe play to go to the West End . . . so bright lights big city here I come! I do still get the odd music royalty cheque, but it's a lucky dip what each one will be depending on whose been playing my songs in the Philippines or Taiwan this month. Maybe I should move to where my loyal fans are in the Far East? Of course, I wouldn't as although my mum is now OK-ish with the carers coming in and out, and me shooting straight back home when I can, my heart and guilt couldn't take being that far away across the world from her. My aunty has gone beyond her call of duty, being the main one who has arranged everything regarding Mum's care plan and checks in on her daily. With my sister living so far away too, I need to stay as accessible as I can regarding any work opportunities that may come in. So back to me becoming a cat. Frida first called me Kav, as most people do, then that became Kavvy the more we spent time together, then, after watching me drunkenly devour her home-made pot of beef stew she announced I reminded her of Garfield the cartoon cat, hence 'Katty' was born.

Tonight Katty has been a bad little kitty after coming home late to Frida's flat due to having to schmooze at a

Variety Club do I got invited to. I had arranged to come to Frida's for the home-made chunky stew sleepover earlier in the day but then got the charity invite and, now I'm treading the boards in a play, thought she may understand my predicament, having to make the executive career decision to go to the ball and have a quick glass of fizz and a few pap shots, which I did with a woman from *Gogglebox* and a runner up from *The X Factor*. I arrived back at Frida's after the long walk from the tube in the rain to be met with her fuming while sat chain-smoking in the dark except for the TV showing the snooker on mute.

'You said you'd be home for my stew. Been out with your *friends,* have ya?'

Hell hath no fury like a woman scorned, especially one that's got a home-made pillowcase with your face on it.

'Oh, I . . . I . . . my battery went flat and I thought you'd be proud of me going to network?'

With that, I leave Frida to her silent snooker and slink off to bed, grateful that I am busy at the theatre for the next few days and then planning a trip back home.

I hear how absolutely fucking insane this sounds – me, who in Frida's eyes is someone she's bought CDs of and has a fan page called 'Faithful Frida 4 Kav', having to explain myself – but I can't really say a word because I'm out of options and I actually enjoy her company. Is this one of them Munchausen cases? Or is it Stockholm? Where the victim falls for their captor? I don't exactly dislike having a warm place to stay where I get well-fed and, more to the point, have two bottles of Aldi's finest chilling for me in the fridge. It's not exactly *Misery*, is it? Not yet anyway. I am grateful for our friendship, though, genuinely, we laugh a lot and there is comfort in knowing someone has my back and cares for me, that is until I receive an email after me taking a bit of a 'break' from our friendship. Frida was not happy with me taking such a wide berth it seems, sending the email at 2am, which I see the following morning sat on the Megabus up north to visit Mum, and simply saying:

> *Dear Katty,*
> *Bang Bang.*
> *You're dead.*

I haven't heard from her since, yet there is still a part of me that misses our bond, which may say more about my issues than dear Frida's.

MORNING MIRACLE

April, 2012

Easter Sunday – the day of resurrection. The only thing I have risen from is the damp, crumpled Egyptian cotton sheets in the guest room of my old stylist friend Dave's new condo in LA, after arriving late last night from London on a flight I have no memory of being on, and that he kindly paid for. This also happens to be the day I will attend my very first Alcoholics Anonymous meeting. In some twisted cosmic joke, I have been dragged back to the city I fled five years ago to face my past and apparently get sober.

Last weekend I was wandering the streets of Majorca, drunk on surgical spirit from the local *farmacia*, after I was kicked out of my Spanish boyfriend Paco's flat, having gone there to salvage what was left of the crumbling long-distance relationship I found myself in after meeting him in a nightclub in Brighton on a trip visiting my old backing dancer and lifelong friend Clare who lives there. Sensible, handsome Paco – yet another totally unrealistic suitor for me to hold emotionally hostage with my well-meaning but ultimately destructive ways and car crash of a life – had finally had enough after a week of me professing my undying love while I promised never to drink again while secretly doing just that while he was at work – as a school teacher, I might add.

Back to the medical booze – I was drinking the poisonous liquid because I was down to my last 10 euros and needed something cheaper yet stronger than beer to take the edge off my heartbreak. I have a physical need for alcohol, which I am still in denial of, and anything that says '100 per cent proof' on the bottle will do just that. I saw the stuff when I originally went in to get a bandage for my knee after falling over, and the warped genius in me decided this would be the thing to ease every aspect of my pain, which it did, while no doubt rotting my insides. I reached out to Dave via a series of SOS Facebook messages at the airport after being dumped there, revealing what a pitiful state my life had become, and he decided the right thing to do was to help me.

'You used to pay my wages when I was your stylist, and I made a lot of money,' he said. Such is the chaos or, as I like to call it 'variety', of life lately, I accepted his offer and here I am.

Dave, my once partner in debauched London partying in the late nineties, has since cleaned up his act and is now reaping the personal and professional benefits of being a few years sober. It's no coincidence that the majority of people who get sober go on to do great things. Judging by his current client list of some of the biggest names in American music and film and his now calm, optimistic demeanour, this new sober lifestyle for him has worked.

Meanwhile, I'm locked in his bathroom, shaking and dry-heaving while Dave prepares eggs and English muffins in the kitchen before my very first AA meeting that he will take me to. Even the smell of coffee that's brewing is inducing holy terror, and caffeine would surely bring on a heart attack. I know all too well by now what would fix this misery – a drink. But Dave's is a dry house, not even a stray bottle of cooking wine in sight. I know this because during my sloppy, grateful arrival speech I gave to Dave and his new boyfriend in the kitchen last night, I scoped out every countertop followed by the cupboards and fridge once they went to bed. The result was nothing. I did learn that kombucha has 0.1 per cent alcohol in it, though, but I'd need a vat of it to even touch the sides.

The all-too-familiar panic is overwhelming – skin crawling, heart racing – but underneath it there's a flicker of weird excitement. That part of me that knows how quickly everything will fade the moment I get my fix, which is the only thread of hope I have right now.

'Fifteen minutes, Kav,' Dave calls out from the kitchen.

Sweet Jesus. Fifteen minutes to what? The eggs? Or until we leave for the meeting?

'OK,' I croak back, realising it's more likely to be the meeting he means, as it starts at 11:30am and it's now just turned 11, and it's close by. My mind races. I could leg it down Laurel Canyon to the liquor store I copped was still there last night, but I came with no money. Dave has promised to help me financially while I'm here and told me 'not to worry about a thing', but I can't ask him for money now without raising suspicion. Desperation takes over as I carefully open the drawers by the sink to see if there's any prescription meds Dave or his boyfriend take, preferably anything of the benzo family, like Valium or even a sleeping pill, *anything* to take the edge off. Nothing, though, only a bottle of Advil and some antihistamines labelled 'May cause drowsiness'. *Pathetic.* I need more confirmation than a 'may'. My heart sinks further when I see even the mouthwash teasing me with its jolly 'Alcohol free!' logo. *Fuck you, exclamation mark.*

For a split second I consider the bleach under the sink. *Does that have alcohol in it?* I snap out of my insanity when by some dark miracle the thought occurs to me – aftershave.

There's a cabinet I haven't checked yet, which I open slowly to reveal quite the selection, from Tom Ford to Dior, but each one has a spray nozzle on top which is pointless. Then at the far back I see a half empty bottle of Joop, no spray attached and totally drinkable. Typically, it had to be the most pungent, campest of scents and the one you can smell a mile away. Still, beggars can't be choosers. The purple bottle stares at me like it knows exactly what kind of desperate low I've now sunk to. Fingers shaking as I unscrew the cap, the sickly sweet scent hitting my nostrils. It's disgusting, but I'm too far gone to care.

I wait for a second, imagining how this would look in a movie: the tragic alcoholic downing aftershave in a posh LA bathroom. I laugh at my reflection, what a joke, except the punchline is my life. The taste is beyond description, like someone's melted a plastic Christmas tree with battery acid and marzipan. Immediately I gag, my body repulsed against yet another foreign liquid, but I force it down. One gulp. Two. I can't do a third.

It burns all the way down to my stomach. The shaking in my hands slows to a faint tremor and the palpitations that felt like they were happening anywhere I have skin start to slow. The nausea's still there, but I'm used to that. At least this morning's horror show is on a hopefully long commercial break. I rinse my mouth with water and brush my teeth again, gargling with the mouthwash I no longer resent, now I've found my little helper. A small victory in a brutal morning, one more tiny escape for now. I gently place the aftershave in the same spot I found it and take one last shaky deep breath before heading towards the kitchen.

'How are you feeling?' Dave asks, knowing it's a loaded question, but said with empathy and kindness.

'Getting there,' I whimper with a sorrowful smile, not sure which is worse: the smell of the lukewarm eggs and muffins, or the fact that I just burped Joop.

The sun's way too bright as Dave's jeep rattles down

Laurel Canyon. Each bump in the road sends jolts through my body, threatening to projectile vomit the toxic aftershave cocktail sloshing around in my gut. This is no time to make small talk, so I'm grateful for our history and lifelong friendship which allows us to drive in silence for most of the journey.

'Nearly there now,' he says.

'Mmm-hmm,' I answer back, keeping my lips sealed like a ventriloquist without his dummy while I now deal with the mouth sweats that have arrived right on time for the meeting.

'Amos is looking forward to meeting you,' says Dave.

Jesus Christ. Who's Amos? What is this, a Bible study group too?

'Cool,' I reply. The build-up of spittle is now full-on foam in my mouth. One-syllable replies are all I can muster.

'Remember I told you last night? Amos is a recovery mentor and is going to help you too. He's the coolest guy, don't worry!

Sweet Lord above. This is way too much information for my battered mind to take in. Not only do I have to possibly announce myself to a group of Yankee recovering alcoholics, but I may now be spilling my soul to a complete stranger. What was that about variety again?

The well-needed trip is the perfect tonic, and to say Dave throwing out such a lifeline saved me at a time I could not have sunk lower would be an understatement. Unfortunately, right at the end of my trip, and on the

89th day of my almost 90 days clean and sober, I fuck things up in true self-sabotage mode and relapse the night before I fly home, for no real reason apart from the obvious one that I am an alcoholic still clearly in denial – a drunk, shameful disappointment to not only Dave and all my new friends in recovery out in LA but to myself. The shitshow is back in full swing with bells on, and it has no desire to stop anytime soon . . .

NO PLACE LIKE HOME

My appointment with Janine, my newly appointed work coach at the Manchester Mosley Street job centre, is at 10:30am. It's a place I never imagined I would ever step foot in, yet here I am, finally at rock-bottom, game over. I am stressed and miserable, and if misery loves company then by the look of the people standing in line with me on this sweltering July morning we have certainly found our tribe.

Considering it's still early, or at least to me it is, this place is a circus, but there are no clowns to send in to save me this time. I had to reschedule my original appointment with Janine as I chickened out with nerves at the last minute and didn't have enough bus fare. To be honest, I didn't have enough for booze *and* bus fare, and there was no way on God's earth I could attempt doing this sober. I made sure I had enough money today, though, to buy a four-pack of cheap cider to get myself here.

I've already drunk two cans in the M&S food hall toilets before I arrived, which makes a change from hiding in a back alley, or if I'm lucky a phone box, plus it's really fancy in those toilets. I can also use their own-brand tester aftershave to disguise the smell of the drink, rather than have to go into Boots and spray theirs like I usually do. All the little tricks I've had to learn that come with managing daytime drinking have now crept into my morning routine, too.

I've been too embarrassed or, if I'm honest, full of pride to get any help from the government so far. Maybe it's because I still cling on to the hope that I'll get a new record deal or a life-changing opportunity from my long-time agent Jane, but even she doesn't take my calls anymore and it's obvious that her assistant Christopher, the ex-actor, hates me and probably doesn't even pass my messages on half the time. I shouldn't be so embarrassed, though. This benefits thing is supposedly there to help people when they are out of work, but the word 'seekers' throws me a little. Everyone here looks like they work normal jobs. I'm not sure how it's going to look when I try to explain to Janine that my last job was being a pop star, I've only ever 'worked' at McDonald's, I have no qualifications and what I'm really seeking is a fucking miracle.

Things weren't so good at home with Mum last night, either. She's now not letting the daytime carers do their job by refusing to shower when they attempt to take her for one. This means that when she pees herself and forgets to wash it off it smells bad. She also stops them from changing the bedding in her room when I'm not there, saying, 'Anthony will do it, love.' But Anthony sometimes forgets to do it because he's had too much to drink after a stressful day of taking her to the market in her wheelchair or going to bingo even though she doesn't even know how to play anymore. Anthony would rather sit watching *Deal or No Deal* with her while she repeats herself, not have to clean piss-stinking bedding.

I think the dementia is getting worse, too. She was adamant last night that Noel Edmonds – the presenter of the show – is not the regular host, and after she asked me for the seventh time where the real presenter was, I snapped and said she knows he is the real presenter and will she stop and that I was sick of it. She burst into tears and told me my father would never shout at her like that (I wasn't shouting, I was slurring) if he was alive. She's right. My father would never have shouted at her because he wasn't a shouter. It was her that did the shouting, usually panicking that he'd put the co-codamol painkillers she was addicted to somewhere she couldn't find, or that she's terrified of the tree in the garden smashing through the patio windows – all things she would catastrophise over that were in her head, which was probably the early signs of this illness we are now both having to deal with.

It's best that I go into the kitchen when she cries, as whatever I say to her to attempt to comfort her she forgets five minutes later and is back repeating the same question while I pour another drink and the cycle continues until it's bedtime. We still say our routine goodnight, though, even if we have had a fight over something. Mum doesn't brush her teeth anymore, but even in my mentally exhausted wine haze, I just about manage it before I turn the landing lights out.

'Goodnight and God bless, Mum.'

'Goodnight and God bless, son.'

At least she still knows who I am. Noel Edmonds is the least of my worries.

* * *

There seems to be a ticket system at the job centre that makes no sense to me, so I look for a kind face that might be able to give me a clue on what the actual drill is in this shuffling, tracksuit-bottomed hell on earth. I have nothing against tracksuit bottoms as I am also, in fact, wearing tracksuit bottoms along with my oversized Nike 'Just Do It' T-shirt (I was in no mood for positive slogans but nothing else was clean) and my baseball cap pulled down to my nose in fear of being recognised. Considering I haven't been on TV for quite some time I do still get recognised, especially in my home town of Manchester, but I tend not to attract the same attention I used to.

Now, it's usually from a concerned onlooker who does a double-take at how pale and heavy I've become and says something they think I may want to hear like, 'I hope you don't mind me asking, but did you used to be the singer, Kavana? What are you up to these days, then? Still doing music?' To which I cheerfully reply with something like, 'I've been living in LA working on a new album and will be making a comeback!' Then they ask for a pic, and I do my usual cheeky-chappy smile, trying not to breathe on them for fear of them smelling the morning wine on me. Then we part, both feeling depressed – them with the shock of what a sorry vision I've become, and me resentful of the fact they said 'used to', which I hear as 'aren't anymore and probably never will be again'.

I finally figure out what to do with my ticket and I wait in the queue for my number to be called. The cider is starting to wear off, which is worrying at it's the 9 per cent stuff that normally keeps me in that sweet spot for longer, but I think it must be a mixture of the nerves and the heat. I'm ticket number 477, which is weird as that's like my birthday – 4th November, 1977. Maybe it's a sign from God I'm on the right path. I can see that ticket number 472 is next to be called on the gigantic computer screen. That means there are five jobseekers to go before me and I've figured out each one takes approximately 8–10 minutes (every second counts when you're waiting for the next drink). This means if I'm quick I could pop to the Tesco Metro across the street and get a miniature wine to top the levels up before I see Janine.

I dig my fingers deep around the front pouch of my backpack for loose change, but all I can find is a pound coin and my headphones. Just as I am about to admit defeat, I remember the secret place I sometimes hide money in. The Gucci glasses case that no longer contains Gucci glasses because I sold them at Cash Converters to buy vodka two months ago. If there was ever a time to ask St Anthony for help, it's now. So, I pray: 'Thank you, St Anthony, for finding me enough money to buy enough wine to last me through the day and give me peace and calm.'

I chew frantically on my super-strong but now tasteless chewing gum and reach down into the main part of the rucksack. I open the glasses case inside the bag, not wanting anyone to think I can afford such extravagant eyewear. There, staring back at me, is a thick golden two-pound coin and not one, but four pound coins. A full bottle of Tesco Villa Maria Sauvignon Blanc is exactly £5.99.

I am saved.

MOTHER AND SON

I'm watching *This Morning* in the new tiny living room of the flat at my mum's new sheltered housing accommodation. My old friend is a guest on the sofa discussing her new play, with the jolly presenters flattering her and her career going from strength to strength as a highly respected actress. I feel proud seeing how far she has come, but also bitter at how far I have sunk. My friend, the actress, now talks in a posher accent, which makes me feel a bit resentful. Why distance yourself from your true roots? I haven't. I did have a slight transatlantic accent after my LA years but not for long, and I'd never have gone on TV talking with one. Not that I've had that many opportunities. I suppose you have to be famous in the first place and I haven't exactly been busy in that department since my prodigal return. It seems Morrissey was right: we do hate it when our friends become successful. I don't hate her, of course, and have no business to. I miss her, that's the real truth of it. Maybe I'll go see her in this play she's promoting. I could get the Megabus to London and stay at the £35-a-night place in Paddington I found, despite the itchy lumps I get the next day. It's not exactly the Dorchester.

I could leave a note at the stage door of the theatre in the afternoon with my number and say something like:

> *Dearest friend,*
> *I'm seeing the show tonight by myself and would love to come say hello after?*
> *Understand if you're busy, of course!*
> *So proud of you.*
> *Your old pal,*
> *Anthony*
> *(aka 'Kavana' since we last spoke, ha ha)*
> *xxx*

It's important I put 'Kavana' and not just my surname as then she will be reminded I have been a successful pop star, and I know all too well what it's like having people wanting to say hello after the show. Makes me less needy and things more equal, you see. Then she could text me, ideally before the show, and arrange to see me after it in her dressing room. We could go for a drink, just the two of us. So many memories to catch up on. *I'll need to make sure I just get enough alcohol in me to feel good (pardon the pun!) just before we meet. Not drunk, just confident and calm. I must make sure there's a Tesco nearby in case I need to top up there to save on theatre bar prices.*

* * *

My mother applies another layer of mascara and bronzer on her white complexion in the kitchen mirror. We are due to go to the shops where I will take her in the taxi with the new free wheelchair we have been given while she recovers from the hip operation she finally got round to having after Dad died, and will be using the free taxi vouchers she receives with her sickness benefits since she has also been diagnosed with early onset dementia.

'Don't forget to wash the tan off your fingers, Mum,' I tell her.

She won't remember, but I say it anyway. The fingers she uses to apply the matte bronzer are the ones on her left hand, the bent and crooked arthritic ones, so they will be brown all day. Only her face and left-hand fingers will be tanned, making her look a bit like ET. Regardless of her mind, she still takes pride in her appearance. Since my father died her short-term memory is getting worse, and the repeating of questions is like a broken record. When my old school pal who still keeps in touch, Suzanne, asked me how I'm managing and wasn't it time she went into a proper care home, I replied she was no way ready to go into a home, and that I do it because she's my mother and I love her, which is true. I didn't need to mention that since losing the house I bought us I am now homeless on paper and have nowhere else to live, and that I have a daily drinking habit that she funds also. I don't drink to get drunk; absolutely not. I drink to cope. There has been no time to grieve my father's death since it happened not long after losing the house (great timing, Dad) and my sister is in Cornwall and has her own health issues which she's doing her best to hide from me, even though I know. And I need to take the edge off even more now that I'm having to look after and live with Mum. Madness to some, but it works just fine for us, thank you very much. We need each other. I am not her official carer – we have those come in twice a day – but she won't let them do the jobs written on the care plan that they have to tick off, such as preparing meals and personal hygiene.

'Anthony will do it, love. You can go,' she tells them. I roll my eyes with a smile, letting them know it's fine and of course I'll do it and to just tick it off the list anyway. All colluding in the lie that it probably won't get done today, and we will let them give it another go tomorrow when she will refuse again.

We are searching for the Stork margarine, her favourite, mid-aisle of the Moston Asda – the same Asda my mother would take me to as a kid. The same Asda where I'd wait in the music magazine section for an hour while she did the shopping after getting me from school. The same one the women would stop my mum to tell her how spot-on she was with the tea-leaves reading she did for them last time and can they book her again.

'Love that hair colour, Rita,' they would compliment her.

'It's all natural, you know!' she would reply.

Every.

Single.

Time.

The same Asda I haven't properly stepped foot in for over a decade but due to us finding Mum's new place right back in the area we came from, we've come full circle.

We, or I, have the 'taking Mum out shopping' routine down to a fine art now. I'll order the taxi around lunchtime for '15 minutes' time', which will give me enough time to down the half-bottle of white wine on my empty stomach so that it hits all the needed spots, and have one last look around the house before we go. The remainder of the wine will go into the empty orange Lucozade bottle and placed in my rucksack, along with whatever spray I can find to disguise any unwanted smells. Mother's Dove deodorant or Impulse body spray will do if I've run out. I'm not fussy, and anything is better than sweat and wine as it's not just my mother's personal hygiene that isn't being taken care of properly these days. I will put the baseball cap in the bag also in fear of being recognised, but that won't go on until right before we are arrive at the shopping precinct so that I don't look too chavvy for the taxi driver while I'm helping Mum into his car. I panic about the wheelchair not fitting into the back, but by the time the taxi has arrived the massive glugs of wine have hit all the right receptors making me chatty to the driver and fully confident lodging it into the boot. Once I finally get Mum in with the seat belt on, all is right in the world, as the always-reliable wine dopamine floods my system. Mother will ask me where we are going, and I will tell her for the eighth time that it's the market and Asda, and possibly B&M.

'You like B&M, you said.'

'Oh yes, B&M. I like it in there. Where are we going?' she says again, but the repeating is fine now I've got my wine in me. I may even surprise her with a random afternoon bingo visit post-shopping. She *loves* bingo. It's actually quite cosy in there in the afternoon! I will hum along to the taxi radio now I'm feeling happy and present and in my sweet spot, proud of the mother and son duties I'm taking care of. Proud of the bonding taking place between us. I've been away for years with my career, so it's moments like this, real quality time, that are priceless I tell myself, blissfully unaware of the desperate reality, and that's it's perfectly normal for a man my age with no job and an escalating drink problem to be secretly living in an old people's sheltered housing complex with his mother.

REHAB - PART ONE

October, 2017

My ten lives are up. I am done. I need rehab and quick. I also need a small fortune to get into one, with the wait for government-funded ones being six months at least, according to the doctor. But sometimes being delusional and seeing the glass as always half full (just not of booze) can help, so I reach out to as many people as possible, not for money to pay for one – those types of friends are long gone – but to put the feelers out if anyone has any contacts and could put a word in at a treatment centre that accepts broke and also broken ex-nineties pop stars who will promise to pay the fee once he gets sober. I'm desperate, and if I don't stop drinking soon I fear it could be fatal. I just can't stop.

My first text is to my old pal from back in my London party days in the early stages of my career when things were fun, when we could pull all-nighters and crack on with life the next day, unlike now when an all-nighter involve smoking crack, broken limbs and blacking out in Esso garage service stations sat on the toilet. My friend is in recovery, I know this having seen him at one of my failed attempts at going there myself a few years back. I hadn't seen him for ages and stupidly said, 'Hey, Tony! What are you doing here?!' which was obvious considering where we were.

To my surprise and joy, he replies: 'Hey, mate, I know a place called Steps 2 Recovery and it's residential too – give them a call, I've told them about you,' he says in the message. 'Oh wow. Thanks so much, I will,' I reply, shocked at how quick he got back to me and how easy he's making it all sound. Residential?! Is this a miracle? To be honest, I'm more excited at the thought of having somewhere to actually live rather than get sober. Are my prayers being answered this one last time by a benevolent God whose patience must be wearing thin by now? Luckily I'm only on my second bottle of wine, and with it being 2pm the rehab he is suggesting I call is still open for enquiries. I get through to a calm and very compassionate man called Fred who, unfortunately for him, I tell my life story to before realising I just need to fill in a form and make a proper appointment to have what's called 'an assessment'. God knows what else there is to 'assess' after I've just given him the full car crash and chaotic movie treatment of my life down the phone.

'You will need to be a couple of days clean and sober, though, as there will be a drugs and alcohol test, so you really need to start winding it down before.'

Eh? What does Fred mean? Clean and sober *before*? *I thought the whole point of rehab is to do all that stuff there? Is it not like you see in the movies where the desperate friends and family of the alcoholic each read out a letter to their hopeless relative before putting them in the back of a car with their 'one last bottle' to keep them going on the journey to said place? How the fuck do I do this myself? The appointment isn't until a week on Monday, though, so maybe I could?*

I'm in too much of a state and too alcohol-dependant to dare ask any remaining family members if I can stay with them, as with all the goodwill in the world no one wants to deal with a downtrodden drunk, family or not. I'm not a physically aggressive drunk and have never started a fight in my life, but what I lack in that department I make up for with my tongue, apparently turning into a precocious messy child flailing around demanding food and shouting my apparent favourite drunken response to anything – 'How DARE you' – at anyone who comes within walking distance. Also shouting how much I have done for my parents over the years, buying houses and paying for everything like a sloppy woebegone resentful martyr. Aunty Angela has enough on her plate managing Mum's stuff, and if it wasn't for her support and her dealing with the care home's paperwork me and my sister don't know what we'd do. My sister only tells me so much about her cancer scans, too, after being given the all-clear every six months since she had chemo. I just don't know how to cope with all this. I've purposefully hidden away from any other family members as I'm too ashamed for them to see me of late.

By the skin of my chipped front tooth I somehow manage to *reduce* but not stop my alcohol consumption.

Billy is another friend I reached out to, a songwriter who is actually the brother of my long-time friend Lulu, who I've known since I first got into the music business as a kid. She's been a great support and friend but like others has had to love me from afar these past few years because I just won't or am not willing to sort myself out. Billy has suggested in the past I get some help and gladly puts me in touch with a lady at the PRS Foundation who runs the music support fund for songwriters and artists who need some funding or short-term help in a financial crisis. I explain everything to her and tell her my situation and they put me in a B&B for the weekend leading up to my assessment. The idea is that I can gather myself and hopefully just lock myself away for a couple of days and drink plenty of water so I pass the drugs and alcohol test with flying colours. Which I do. Sort of.

'How many hours does it take for alcohol to leave your system?' I google.

I'm sat on the single bed in the little B&B in King's Cross near the PRS office that Christine booked me into. According to Google – I have now reworded this question at least three times in order to find the answer that suits me and will tell me I *can* drink the night before my assessment – for alcohol to leave your system it takes 'anything from 12–24 hours'.

Great. Ish. This means that with my test thing being at 9:15am, if I stay within the safest option of 24 hours, my *last* drink pre-test will have to be at 9:15am tomorrow (Sunday) morning! Which also means to get a good drink in I'll have start at 7am at least! However, if I hedge my bets and go for the 12-hour window I can drink all day but must wrap it up at by, say, midnight. Now half-impressed at my sudden mathematic skills that would give Carol Vorderman a run for her money, I have to make the decision of which option to take. There is no way in my current dependency I can stop at 9:15am tomorrow then go the whole day and night without a drink, so I go for the latter option and just pray I make it out the other side with flying colours, or in my case, booze-free piss.

OSMOSIS

'I feel it in my bones like osmosis,' Sonja says.

Sonja is a German lady who looks like a Bond villain and is one of the residents here at rehab. 'Osmosis' is her new word of the week and I am pretty sure she's using it wrong. Last week's word was 'instinct', which she pronounced 'ink-stink', and we had the same issue then. I first met her when I arrived, when she was sat sulking on the stairs outside counsellor Fred's office after being busted for making out with another resident called Gary in the laundry room. She, like myself, is one of the 'live-ins' here at Steps 2 Recovery rehab, unlike some of the others who are on the day programme and get to go home at 3:30pm. It feels like school, except our teachers are trained psychotherapists and counsellors. They are also ex-addicts who understand what we are going through, rather than having a PhD on addiction like, say the Priory, which none of us could afford anyway. This rehab is mainly for ex-convicts who got clean in prison and then come here after serving time to 'build a bridge to normal living' before going back into the real world. The ones who don't fit that bill, i.e. me and a handful of others, and can't afford private rehab come here because they are either homeless, fucked or both (also me).

After our morning cleaning duties (clean house, clean mind) we gather in the living room where we must attend group therapy sitting in a circle. I hate sitting in circles. I hate sitting in circles even more when I'm less than a week from detoxing from the last almighty binge, which this time culminated in me smoking crack in a skip with a homeless lady who I bonded with then trusted with my Monzo card to go buy more drugs and who never returned. Note to self: never give a stranger your pin code when high, and never do crack because you will want more and it makes you feel like your heart is going to explode after doing so.

Now back to Sonja. She has used the word 'osmosis' approximately four times already in her share, each time using it for different reasons.

'I don't feel safe when Clive keeps pressuring me to use Henry the hoover on the stairs.'

'Why's that, Sonja? Try to go underneath the fear,' Fred our counsellor asks.

'Because he resents my osmosis.'

I wish Fred would just put her out of her misery and ask what she thinks she means by that, but I guess we are not here for our academic qualities. Clive, who Magda has beef with, is a fellow resident here and can be very angry and moody. I think it may be because he's been in prison for such a long time that he's used to things being done a certain way. He has told her several times this week that she is using the hoover incorrectly when it's her turn to do the stairs. Something to do with the lead not being put back right on the 'trunk' as he calls it, which I thought was a term used for elephants only. *How does he know? Surely they don't have Henry the hoovers in prison?* I don't, or more to the point am too scared, to get involved as Clive is also a convicted murderer and I wouldn't want to rub him up the wrong way.

I stare out of the lounge window and start to daydream instead. I sometimes wonder what life would have been like if I hadn't moved to LA all those years ago, when I thought my career was over the first time. Maybe if I'd stuck it out in the UK I'd have had another shot. I could have signed a new record deal or reinvented myself as an actor, like Billie Piper. *She turned it around so why didn't I?* I remember when the two of us opened the rebranded Topshop on Oxford Street. We had to burst through a huge paper sheet in front of hundreds of fans who had lined up to see us. We were laughing because it was too early on a Saturday morning to be having to do such a task and she was laughing even more because my head kept getting stuck. Billie was my friend too, and we were on the same label. She said she fancied me in *Smash Hits* once, and I adored her. If there was any girl pop singer I wish I could have not been gay for if it would have been Billie. Now she's picking up

Bafta nominations and I'm picking up resentments over having to clean the toilet in a government-funded rehab.

'I think we will leave it there for this morning,' Fred says, snapping me out of my daydream to do our final check-in before lunch. 'Are we ready with our one word?'

I hate this bit. We have to go round the circle and each say one word to describe how we are feeling in that exact moment.

'Sonja, let's start with you.'

I anticipate something nonsensical, but she surprises us.

'Forgiveness.' *Blimey, I wasn't expecting that. Maybe this stuff does work.*

'Clive, what's your *one* word to describe how you're feeling right now?'

Fred emphasises the word 'one' as Clive usually gives at least four.

'Hungry,' he says, shrugging his shoulders. I think it's safe to say we are here for the long haul with him.

I zone out while the rest of the group give theirs. *I wonder if Billie would be willing to be friends with me again. Most famous people who I thought were my friends back then don't bother with me these days, and God forbid they follow me back on Instagram.*

'Kav, let's finish with you. What's your word?'

'Hopeful,' I say, more cheerily than I'd planned to. Not because of rekindling an old friendship with an old pop pal which will probably never happen anyway, but because for the first time in years I'm starting to see little possibilities. *How am I learning all this stuff? Maybe Sonja was right, even if she didn't know it.* I guess essentially it's all going into this weary, broken brain of mine by osmosis, and just for today, that's fine by me.

BIRTHDAY BOY

'You do realise it could be seen as grooming?' counsellor Fred says. On my 40th birthday. In rehab. Fred said it. Not me. Fred. Even though I know he's well-trained with people like me and knows not to throw around such a term. I think this word is too strong. I went along with all of it. I liked it.

'But no one forced themselves on me, and I enjoyed it.' This almost feels scripted as it comes out of my mouth, like I'm defending the person he's accusing. 'It's in the past anyway. I'm not a victim.'

Fred pushes his glasses back on his nose as he does when he's about to say something with more weight to it, something I may not want to hear like, 'Admitting you're powerless is the first step to recovery,' the kind of statement that's so fucking obvious is why I've found myself in a residential rehab for homeless people and ex-convicts in the first place.

'You were a child.'

I jump up, a reflex almost, and see the chewing gum I knew I had sat on when our session started but was too embarrassed to move has melted and formed one big white strand stuck to the chair and my tracksuit bottoms, like a rope pulling me back down and forcing me to carry on with this way-too-heavy a conversation to be having at 11:30am on a Monday morning.

'But I was 18 when . . .'

I sit back down, not even bothering to get into it with the chewing gum. I'll deal with it later.

'You *turned* 18 that night, Kav, the night it happened. Do you think it's a coincidence that it wasn't until you were officially legal that something sexual happened?'

I feel my defences drop with this statement. Has Fred got a point? I mean on paper it could look like this, but surely not? Surely it wasn't planned? Surely I wasn't taken away from my own birthday party with the knowledge that anything that happened from that moment on had no repercussions because I was finally classed as an 'adult'? I haven't felt sick for weeks since I detoxed but I suddenly feel a new type of nausea I don't recognise. It's beyond physical, making me feel hopeless and incompetent. A soul sickness, if there is such a thing.

'Look, we've covered a lot today and we are nearly out of time. How are you feeling?'

'It's a lot, yes, but I definitely feel better,' I say, not sure what I'm feeling or, more to the point, want to feel, so I doubt Fred buys it either, but we both know he has a rowdy treatment centre to get back to and we need our lunch before afternoon group therapy begins.

We stand and hug each other.

'Well done, Kav.'

'Thanks, Fred.'

'And happy birthday again! There's a big cake downstairs, a little birdy told me.'

I almost forgot that today is my 40th birthday. I didn't hear him say it before either.

'Oh God. I didn't think I'd be turning the big 4-0 in rehab!' I half joke, two pivotal birthdays now mentioned this morning, 18 and 40, both being ones I won't forget, for very different reasons.

I shove the chair back in the corner and grab a green paper towel from the dispenser and place it over the remaining bits of chewing gum that are stuck to it, while Fred checks the day's rota on his phone and I hope he doesn't see my mess.

'It's going to be OK,' he says.

'Yes,' I reply, my head pounding with the possible realisation of what Fred just told me.

I take one last look at the chair and the paper towel that now hides the chewing gum underneath. Fred hasn't noticed it either. It looks better now. Covered up. A secret.

POST REHAB

Being an ex-nineties pop flop, as I was referred to by a kind Australian journalist once, is no easy job. It requires having to be recognised randomly once a month, usually when you're at your worst, which for me of late is every day of the week, and it also takes some acting. It seems my LA course in the Meisner technique was not a waste after all. It's important to be jolly and grateful, you see, so if you're on a comedown or drunk or worse, you still have to greet your spotter with a cheerful 'Yes, it's me' or 'Thank you' depending on how you're greeted, which can range from 'Are you that singer?' or 'I'm a bit embarrassed to say I loved you once'.

The only time it's a real problem is days like today. Since moving into the bedsit after my rehab stint I have failed to remain sober. I got a little carried away on my return from a music-writing retreat that I was gifted by one of the funders from the rehab after she bid on it at the charity Christmas auction and decided with me being a (newly six-month clean and sober) songwriter she would give it to me. Only problem being that there was so much booze knocking around on the retreat it was constantly in my eyeline, and although I clung on for dear life by not touching a drop while singing our daily songs we had written round the campfire each night, as soon as I got home it was on me like a 500-pound gorilla. So I drank. I initially just had one bottle, which turned into two, and by the time evening came I was back at the off-licence buying Glen's Vodka, which I took it upon myself to drink huge gulps of in the phone box as I couldn't wait to get my fix. Brutal. Since then, the beast has truly been released and with the all the best will in the world I Can't. Stop. Drinking. I'm also supposed to be on the 'day programme' at my rehab which happens *after* your original rehab stint to slowly ween you off the support there before entering real life and AA meetings. Rather than tell dear Fred that I have in fact relapsed I have made the feeble excuse of having flu but am actually on day six of a booze binge that won't stop. The woman in the corner shop has also noticed that my demeanour has changed in the last week, as I have gone from buying tzatziki and lentil chips – my usual pre-TV dinner snack in sobriety – to witnessing me appearing like Nosferatu in an unwashed Primark hoodie the minute she opens at 7am to buy my supplies. The always polite and cheerful woman went from wishing me a good evening to asking 'Are you OK, my dear?' when I stumbled back in for my second three-litre bottle of White Lightning cider I purchased before noon along with a tin of cat food for the cat I don't have, in a failed attempt to lead her off the scent and look like a somewhat responsible pet owner. Madness.

So back to the being recognised. Feeling just the right amount of 'relaxed' and talkative – which by now takes a good three-quarters of 13.5 per cent wine drunk in one go before leaving the house – I take a walk on the high street one sunny day in one of my relapse benders and get chatting to a homeless lady from Dublin named Rita. 'Same name as my mum! It's a sign!' I say, desperate for connection with anyone that won't tell me to stop drinking, which at this point is everyone left in my phone. I see that Rita is also like me possibly, an alcoholic, as she is swigging the very same cheap cider I also have a penchant for, that comes in huge blue plastic bottles and tastes like out-of-date vinegar but, at a pound a litre, beggars can't be choosers, literally. I tell her my name is Anthony rather than 'Kav', mainly because that's what her namesake, my mother, calls me. In her charming and lyrical Dublin accent Rita replies, 'No it's feckin' not, ya bastard! You're dat singer, aren't ya?!' so loud even the queue outside the post office turns round. My mother's posh friend Dorothy once passed out outside the Co-op on a coach-trip pit stop in St Annes, after mistakenly doubling up on her HRT patch, and said 'it was the most embarrassing thing in my life, not even Marks & Spencer's – the CO-OP!' and now I feel Dorothy's pain, as being recognised by a sozzled Irish woman sat on the street outside Iceland has to be an all-time low even by my standards.

'Shhh,' I say to Rita, in the hope that she won't bring any attention to local shoppers who may wonder who in fact she is referring to. 'Keep your voice down.' At which point the realisation is complete and Rita announces to the high street:

'You're dat Kavana!'

I'm not sure what's worse, the fact she has outed me on a high street full of now slightly-puzzled shoppers who are still none the wiser even with the name announcement, or that she see referred to me as 'that' which is what I'm assuming she said, it's hard to tell with such a thick accent.

I tell Rita I'll see her in a bit and hotfoot it into the Wetherspoons opposite for a top-up to ease the embarrassment and pray that when I come out she's either found a new spot to settle in for the day or that she will also be too drunk to care.

After a slow walk round Savers to purchase floor wipes and an Air Wick stench-neutralising candle (booze and sweat won't leave your living quarters without assistance), I cross over to the small park behind the high street. It's a quiet spot where one can sit and while away the hours if the weather is decent, which today it is, with a late autumn sun making the flowers on the mini allotment glow up a bright yellow.

I crack open another 7 per cent beer and wonder what Dad, wherever he is, thinks of this mess I've got myself in. His last words of 'Aren't you lonely, son?' ringing in my ears. I am. Yes. But I can't do much about that today.

A SADNESS

I have a sadness I can't explain. A constant low-level feeling of dread, a yearning for something, a malady of sorts. For as long as I can remember I've been trying to ease this feeling, but nothing sticks. No person, no place, and no amount of success has quenched my constant thirst for more. More love, more joy, more approval, more touch. I'd say more money, but that never really did it for me, apart from when I find myself really desperate like last week, for example, when I was scraping the top drawer for silver coins to buy my morning booze and, of course, the cat food. Let's not forget the cat food. As I mentioned before – a gentleman must never buy booze at that time on its own. Too suspicious. A tin of mid-range (not Whiskas) such as Felix does the job. This usually puts the shop owner off the alcoholic's scent, you see. They don't need to know that there is no cat waiting for her breakfast at home. I really must go to the local foodbank to donate the ever-mounting tins I have under the sink, but last time I went there I was rude to the support volunteer when she was trying to palm me off with marrowfat rather than garden peas. I know beggars can't be choosers but why would anyone want to chew on a hard pea when we have the sweet soft ones that are the garden variety? Speaking of garden variety, if I hear one more person say in a recovery meeting, 'I'm nothing special, I'm just a garden-variety drunk,' I swear I'll walk out. No, Mr, you're not a garden-variety anything, you're a basic self-righteous drunk who happens to have got some years off the drink under your belt by clinging on for dear life and coming here to moan about it. Needless to say I've been slack on going to meetings. 'The only rule in AA is the desire to stop drinking,' or so I'm told, but I don't have the desire to stop – that's the problem. It's got its grip again and I'm fucked if I know how to quit. I'm back to isolating in the flat and not answering the phone to well-wishing but what I assume to be currently, nosy 'fellows' from AA.

THE ROAD TO RECOVERY (SORT OF)

*P*eople, *places and things, oh my . . . People, places and things, oh my!*

I'm skipping down the high street like a manic but sober alcoholic, also known as a 'dry drunk', i.e. someone that isn't doing 'the work', which makes me eyeroll every time I hear it. 'It wasn't until I did the work that I found true relief from my self-centred fear.' Whatever! I'm giggling to myself at some of the sayings I hear at the 12-step meetings I now have to attend in order to stay sober on a daily basis, which I'm not. My *Wizard of Oz* lions, tigers and bears-inspired chant is in relation to one, or three in this case, of the many triggers that can affect us or me on my so called new journey of self-discovery and sobriety. I thought once I put down the drink all would be fixed, but oh no! You see, when you put down your medicine or, let's say, anaesthetic – which for someone like is me is alcohol and more recently the odd bit of crack, but let's not confuse the real issue here (booze) – you are left with 'feelings', which for someone like me who has blurred them out for 30 years due to a heady mix of shame, guilt, self-obsession, grief, loss of fame and throw in a bit of sexual trauma while we're at it, means you are now left completely raw, hence the other slightly annoying but very true statement you hear in the rooms of AA: 'The good thing about being sober is you get your feelings back, the bad thing about being sober is you get your feelings back.' Shame they didn't add 'fucking' before the second use of feelings in the statement. These 'feelings' that can now erupt at any given moment, having been drowned and quelled by the booze, can – according to those in the know – be triggered by three main things: People. Places. Things.

People

These could be anyone from your past or present that may still trigger you who you may have had to drink just to be around at times, or that made it easier for you to continue your addiction, even if they didn't mean to. People you now realise you were in toxic relationships with – romantically or as friends – those that caused emotional stress or resentment and instability which can make a person vulnerable to relapse. Even after amends are made with those we may have hurt through our addictions, just because the addict has done the work on themselves it soon becomes quite clear in recovery who from your past now has good intentions and who doesn't. It's not about suddenly being the 'better person' and shutting the door on them, it's about healthy boundaries and ultimately staying alive.

Places

So, for example, when I would visit my mum in the care home and witness her not recognising me and start to feel the absolute heart-sinking feeling that brings when looking into the eyes of the woman who raised you – and saved up bus fare to take you to piano lessons in the rain, the same woman who idolised you since birth and would literally die for you – and drawing a blank in return, I could run to the toilet in the care home as I did on many occasions and slug vodka so I didn't have to 'feel' that heartache. *And* it would also allow me to spend more quality time with my mother who doesn't recognise me. Surely that's a win?

Things

These can include anything, such as copious amounts of empty wine and vodka bottles that no longer fit under the sink and end up 'hidden' in drawers or under the bed, the joke being the only person they are being hidden from is yourself. Seeing these could bring on shame or a craving. The idea is to empty them as you go, but when you're living in a tiny studio flat on the top floor the clinking of the bottles while trying to get to the bin and not be spotted by a neighbour can be too much to handle, especially if you can't stop shaking. Even clothes can set off an addict trying to stay sober. I wore the same red Adidas tracksuit bottoms for the best part of month on one of my last binges – I even slept in them. When the thought of even brushing your teeth leaves you in fear of choking on one more morning dry-heave over the sink, clothes are the least of your worries. The tracksuit bottoms were in such a state by the end, covered in booze, sweat, dried noodles and cigarette burns, a dear no-nonsense friend named them my 'relapse trousers', i.e. if I had them on it was a sure sign it wasn't just peach Oasis I was slugging at a meeting.

The one thing I *do* appreciate about AA is that it clearly states: 'The only requirement for AA is the desire to stop drinking,' which means if I am still drinking or, let's face it, can't stop drinking, I'm still allowed entry. Almost like some secret underground spiritual club of people who know the secret to living happy and free from booze – I'm just not sure what that is yet.

It doesn't say 'today' or 'forever', so for now this is what keeps me going. I keep being told by these well-meaning but surely lying types that 'you'll never need to drink again' but they are missing the point. I *do* want to drink again! I just want to be able to drink normally, that's all.

There's no doubt they are good people, but if I was truly honest my suspicions may have led me to believe they are a bit naive, though. All this 'handing it over to a god of your understanding to keep you sober' business seems a stretch. It's something to do, I guess, as there are so many meetings that I can spend my days going from one to the next, which I do. Unfortunately for me, though, my rock bottom isn't quite ready for me, and I'm still hovering comfortably numb above it. It's called the 'gift of desperation' in the rooms of recovery, and you'd think becoming homeless and ending up in a government-funded rehab would have done the trick but it hasn't. That gift has been tossed to one side like a toddler does after opening its shiny wrapped presents on Christmas day. I, like the toddler, have got my prize, the rest, just like the wrapper, was the means to an end to get me here. I got a little place to live with a sink and a bed, and I am happy for the most part, as long as I have enough money to buy my drink and cigarettes and food in that order. I'll get sober in my own time. When *I'm* ready.

ANGELA

My best friend, who also happens to be my sister, and I are sat in our usual spot in deck chairs on Porthminster Beach in St Ives, Cornwall. I'm on a new round of sobriety and feeling somewhat hopeful, so a trip to see Angela and Clint feels like the break and catch-up that's needed. I've been coming to St Ives since I was a child, since Angela and Clint moved here in the late eighties. A home from home, filled with some of the happiest memories I have. Being born 20 years after my sister, we never had that sibling rivalry some brothers and sisters may have – there was never any fighting over toys as kids or any jealousy over which parent loved who the most, instead she has always been my friend, someone I look up to and feel excitement to be around. Angela: the life and soul of any party, a life force that hits you the second she walks into the room. Big blue eyes and jet black hair, with a warmth and sense of humour like no other. It's been a rough few years for my sister, not that she lets on or tells me too much, but now, after finishing her second round of radiation after having cancer a few years ago, I've noticed a change in her. It's hard to discuss the truth regarding the cancer as it's like she doesn't want to burden me, instead staying upbeat and her usual self when she's feeling good and then goes quiet when I assume she's not.

Her and Clint living in Cornwall has always meant you can't just pop round unannounced either, not that she'd like that anyway. Angela is either 100 per cent in your company or not at all. It's either laughter, deep conversations and quality time or nothing, and since she's been given the all-clear for what she says is another six months, she suggested I make my at-least yearly trip to Cornwall. We like to sit in our favourite spot, right opposite the beach café, with the Tate museum looking down from above that. She's not been on the beach much this summer, she says, which gives me a clue that she hasn't been feeling great. Clint is a hairdresser and his salon in Penzance was always a hub of excitement I would spend days in as a curious teenager, fascinated by the weird and wonderful customers he would cut the hair of while Angela took charge of the reception, chatting away to the customers and offering them Douwe Egberts coffee and the latest copy of *Hello!*. Clint has since sold the salon and gone mobile, so Angela now runs all his appointments each morning from their bedroom overlooking the harbour. Her 'boudoir', as she likes to call it. Today we are playing our favourite game where we take it in turns to spot a holidaymaker or a family on the beach and create stories about each one for entertainment, the more bizarre the better.

'See her over there in the leopard-print two-piece?'

'Go on,' I'll say, knowing that whatever tale she's going to concoct is about to have us both laughing for the next half an hour, after which, now egged on by my hilarious sister, I will attempt to go one better with whichever poor bugger I can spot.

'See that man over there eating the pasty behind the windbreak with the comb-over?'

'Oh, aye,' she'd say, and the game continues until our bellies hurt from laughing or a wild seagull has swooped and snatched one of her home-made pittas we brought in our packed lunches, probably as karma for our made-up stories about innocent holidaymakers.

Among the laughter, though, there is a worry for each other, hers for me regarding my drinking and my chaotic life. I thought it would be a tricky one to navigate with her, the whole stopping-drinking thing, especially since Angela and Clint are my best friends, really, which means they have of course been a part of my drinking life. That's what we do together and have done since I've been old enough *to* drink. We've spent hundreds of nights together talking over bottles of wine, they've seen me at my most 'successful', buying houses and quaffing champagne with the best of them, but it always comes back to just the three of us – my safety net. They've been with me through every high and every low, every hard decision I've had to make, every heartache, met partners, even trodden lightly but in no uncertain terms told me who I should steer clear of and were usually always right after me finding out the hard way for myself. So now with my new life in sobriety it feels selfish to me that our mutual love for a drink – the thing that at times connects us and has always been there through thick and thin – has been taken away. I am raw and my sister has cancer – how do I even begin to find a way to discuss it with her when my anaesthetic for everything has been taken away? The selfishness of me even thinking this makes me feel disgusted with myself. It feels like my nerves are on the outside of my body at times and I'm constantly in fight or flight. With Dad gone, Mum being diagnosed with actual Alzheimer's and in the care home, and now my sister's cancer, I'm swimming against the tide of bad luck. At least I have a chance to get better – I just stop drinking. Angela has to make the best of these six-month windows she gets the all-clear from. I really need to get a grip. I'll never forgive myself if I relapse again.

'Come on, cock. We're going in.'

My sister snaps me out of my mental melodramas to announce she is going in the sea and wants me to go in with her. Nice try, sis. I know what she's up to. She knows I can't bear the icy cold water on this beach. I'm in awe of her bravery, though, not just going in the water but the real thing she's been facing. It seems she's made of the same stuff our dad was. Always finding humour, no matter what.

'You go, I'll mind the stuff!' I say, half wanting to join her but not wanting to spoil her apparent childlike excitement. She loves the water. She's a brilliant swimmer too. Won the gold medal at the school swimming galas, she said. I might not even be here if it wasn't for Angela, as on my first holiday down here with Mum and Dad, and not long after they'd moved here, when I was about eight years old, we hired a big rubber dinghy and went in the sea. Mum stayed on the beach as she hated the water. She sat there with her tights on her head waving us off. The dinghy tipped over past the buoys as the force of the current pushed us over and I sank all the way to the bottom. I can remember seeing my fringe float up and down in slow motion while Angela, Clint and Dad were apparently screaming my name and diving under but couldn't find me. Amid the sheer panic and mayhem, Angela said she just took a massive breath and bolted herself down under the water, spotted me, and scooped me up under her arm and dragged me and her to the shore. I coughed up seaweed while everyone else fell to their knees in relief. We all agreed not to tell Mum, who was oblivious eating a beef-paste butty on the sand, waving to us as we caught our breath walking back up the beach.

'Oh, come on. It's lovely once you're in! I've not been able to go in this summer with one thing and another, why don't you just dip your feet in, you silly fool?!'

I almost say yes, but something inside, a hunch, wants me to stay and watch her.

'I tell you what, you go and see how bloody cold it is first and then I'll decide, plus I can mind our stuff.'

With that she pulls that knowing cheeky Angela

face, wraps her sarong round her now smaller waist and slowly marches down to the shore. I want to take a photo of her walking down the beach on her first visit into the sea in a long time, but I know she hates having her picture taken. God knows why because she's stunning. Clint said when he first laid eyes on her she reminded him of a young Ava Gardner, although I've always thought she looks more like Elizabeth Taylor with those sapphire-blue eyes.

I try to spot her but all I can see is heads bobbing up and down. Then, right on cue as the late afternoon sun bursts through one of the clouds, I see someone waving further out against the now golden lit water. I know it's her as I can make out her purple swimsuit and big smile. There she is. My brave sister, letting me know she made it to the ocean, looking completely at peace and in her happiest place, almost childlike. I wave back and then she disappears again, diving right under the ocean. Gone, into the vast deep blue. Unbeknown to me this will be our last time together on this beach that holds a thousand memories, so I don't take a picture. I don't need to, it's tattooed in Technicolor in my mind, and on my heart forever.

* * *

12 months later

'Here he is, Elvis!' exclaims Margaret, homeless pal of Rita's, and the woman who robbed me of 20 quid before I went into rehab after I gave her my Monzo card to get cash out (as you do) to buy 'two white, one dark' and then taking me to one of her secret places for us to smoke it – a skip on a housing estate in Hackney. I'm not sure what baffles me more: her absolute cockiness about taking an extra 20 quid from my account and stealing my card, or that she called me Elvis, a backhanded compliment if ever there was one. The only Elvis I have any visual similarities too is the bloated and sweating one circa Vegas '77, not long before he left the building for good.

'Fancy a smoke, Antnee?' asks Irish Rita, my more trustworthy drug-taking companion, and she doesn't mean the ordinary cigarette or spliff variety. How these people keep going living on what appears to be a 99 per cent drug diet, I've no idea. I also have no idea how they can do this stuff day-in day-out without ever wanting to give it a rest. Maybe they, like me with alcohol, need the stuff to function? But surely topping up your levels with a few bottles of wine or beer or whatever is different than topping up with class A drugs that blow your socks off and send your brain into Jupiter after one hit? Then there's the comedown. Never mind 'Suicide Tuesday', it's a full week at least of the darkest paranoia and palpitations, and that's even with drinking in an attempt to soften the comedown blow.

'No, not tonight, I'm being good,' I hear myself say, realising I have absolutely no idea who or what I've become. Like it's normal to say to your new pal, the well-meaning drug addict who's begging on the street, that you might just be taking it easy tonight from, you know, smoking crack. Like someone who's on a diet who coyly tells their friend they won't be having any chocolate, or that cheeky glass of wine once the kids have gone to bed.

I give Irish Rita a smile and keep walking, ignoring Margaret.

I wonder if maybe she did mean the younger Elvis, though?

I have started to get back into the AA meetings and try with all my might to really stick to it this time. I can't seem to understand, though, how I can feel like I'm doing well and doing all the right things suggested by my now third sponsor – after the last one fired me when I mentioned my last relapse involved drugs *and* booze – and then have this almighty craving out of nowhere, which like a magnet or some crazy blind spot has me picking up the first drink again. At first I was pretty angry when the last sponsor told me he couldn't work with me as he thought the whole point of AA was based on rigorous honesty – which I thought me telling him about my drug escapades in the skip was being just that – but maybe some sponsors can only handle a sponsee (me) that has alcohol issues? I don't see myself as a drug addict which is why I don't go to NA meetings, but then again isn't alcohol a liquid drug? Oh, I don't know. I just feel rejected, I suppose. It seems the saying is right: alcohol and drugs do make people leave, even your guiding light of a sponsor in my case.

DIVINE TIMING

I'm charging my phone in the plug socket in what I call my new office, Costa Coffee on the high street in Hackney. A whole year has gone by, of some months of sobriety and meetings and trying my best to stay sober but always ending up back at rock bottom. I've been drinking now for three months straight and have lost contact with those I love. I've come to my new office after drinking my first three-litre bottle of white cider, which at £3.99 is a bargain, and after vomiting the first few mouthfuls back up – my body rejecting it instantly until it finally surrenders to let it stay down and do its job – I stop shaking and sweating enough so that I can leave the house and get some fresh air. I haven't showered in days and my hair is matted with my scalp covered in broken skin, flakes of it constantly falling on whichever hoodie doesn't smell the worst, as the desire to wash my clothes has also gone. A merry-go-round of dirty laundry and a hotch-potch of outfits to wear under my big charity-shop-bought winter coat that just about fits round my alcohol-bloated stomach. After I manage to drink the gallon of cider, and feeling somewhat human again, I head over to the Co-op and buy a bottle of their cheapest but strongest white wine along with a small bottle of water before heading to my office and ordering a black Americano, mainly so I can have the paper cup. I will then go into the hopefully unoccupied toilet and pour the coffee immediately down the toilet. I try not to catch a glimpse of the tragic puffy-faced figure I have become in the bathroom mirror until I drink half the bottle of wine down in one go, then fill up the rest with water. I then carefully pour a cup of my new wine/water mix into the paper cup and go back to my seat in the corner at the back. I sit and scroll through the missed calls and unopened messages and sip the cup, cleverly blowing on it as if it's hot coffee so no one suspects until I feel relaxed enough to plan whatever the day's itinerary could entail. On this particular day, and for reasons unbeknown to me at the time, I decide to check my emails. Not that I get any these days apart from the usual spam or Spotify artists' email telling me to update my artist page with gig info and new releases, which won't be happening any time soon. If I'm feeling extra confident I may go onto my artist's page to see how many people are listening in that very moment, and it always seems to say, 'You have 28 people listening now.' I wonder who these kind fans are and wonder what they would think if they knew that while they were humming or singing along to one of my songs, the very artist they are listening to is drinking booze in a high-street coffee chain with a smashed phone screen to match his mind at 9:20am.

'Hi, Anthony. Please can you call me, I'm trying to get hold of you,' reads the email marked 'Urgent' from a lawyer who reached out to me a year ago after a heads-up from a former pop pal regarding some kind of defamation case in the nineties. I remember talking to this lawyer, luckily in one of my more lucid moments, but have heard nothing since. I just assumed I was too young to have any newspapers sniffing around me or attempting to hack my phones in my pop years so forgot all about it. Any stories that have come out in the press since then were much later and usually booze-related: 'Nineties pop star drunkenly falls off stage at Butlin's' being one of my not so finest moments in recent years.

I call the lawyer back and she tells me that my case was valid and that the newspaper in question have settled, culminating in me being paid an amount of money I haven't seen in well over a decade. Apart from falling off my chair and almost collapsing with shock, gratitude and amazement, the second I get off the phone I call my latest AA sponsor, Ricky, a kind and wise American man who has stuck by me the last year, and never judged me when I refused to follow some simple steps and do the work on myself in order to stay sober, always thinking I know best and always ending up back where I started except ten times worse. I tell him I want to go to a private rehab and can he please help find me one somewhere. At this point I'm so full in my addiction I need a medical detox with the possibility of it being fatal if I stop suddenly on my own, not that I could anyway. I take this financial miracle as a sign and surely my last chance to give myself a shot at getting sober. With the help of Ricky and some AA friends who have to spend the next two days going back and forth to A&E to get the all-clear with bloods and paperwork for me to enter the facility, I arrive on the Friday for a month's stay. Once the fog clears after one of the most brutal detoxes I've ever been through, I start to feel more alive than I've felt in a long time and start putting the work in I need to, determined that this time will be the one that sticks.

RETURN TO OZ

2023

Not long after my one-year sobriety date, I take a trip up north by myself to go see my mum.

I notice how different I feel – calmer and more relaxed rather than dreading it in case Mum doesn't recognise me. I meet one of Mum's new carers, a cheerful woman called Glinda who jokes she's the 'good witch of the home'. I laugh to myself – if only she knew my *Wizard of Oz* obsession. Mum sits in her usual chair by the window, only this time she's got a doll on her knee and tells me it's her baby. She's smiling and seems much calmer than when I saw her last. Our eyes meet and I notice how blue they look, and for the first time in a long time I feel like I've come home.

'You alright, Rita?' I say. It's funny, as since Mum has been in the care home and I guess appeared to forget stuff, including that I'm her son, I just one day started calling her by her name, Rita, instead of Mum.

I'm not sure whether it's because I'm holding out for some recognition, as if using her name might spark some distant memory from the past seeing as me calling her 'Mum' just doesn't seem to register. Maybe I want her to remember herself and who she is. Everyone knew Rita. Everyone loved Rita.

'Is that your baby?' I ask her, feeling like a fraud talking to my own mother like she's daft. She must be in there somewhere. I hold her hand while she looks at the baby, smiling, then back up at me and stares right into my eyes.

'You're my baby,' she says. Clear as day.

'I am your baby, aren't I?' I reply, feeling like the happiest son alive.

Glinda tells me a package arrived a few weeks ago addressed to me. I'm slightly baffled to say the least until I open it and it hits me. When I was in Steps 2 Recovery, Counsellor Fred said he had a present for me which he'd give me one day, but for whatever reason either he kept forgetting or I was too wrapped up trying to stay sober to ask. Now, staring back at me, is a copy of the *Smash Hits* cover I did when I was in Italy with the words 'THE RETURN OF KAVANA' in big bold letters on the front. Inside is a little slip of paper with a letterhead from my old rehab that just says: 'To Kav, from Fred.' He must have somehow got a copy and wanted to give it me as a laugh or as a last farewell before I left. God knows I went on enough about being a '*Smash Hits* award winner' to him.

What's even more poignant is that Fred sadly passed

away last year and Steps 2 Recovery closed down a few months ago, so I can only imagine they had Mum's care home address to forward it to with me not having one of my own back then.

It's almost as though he meant for me to have it now instead, when I was doing good and on a better path, even though I don't really know where this one will take me yet.

It could be said I am returning to something. Sanity? Sure. Happiness? I hope so, or is it that I'm returning to myself. The real me who got caught up in a whirlwind and never really found that safe landing until now. As for the future, who knows. One thing I do know is that I have hope, just good old-fashioned hope, and just for today that's good enough for me.

I think of Fred hugging me on my birthday, in rehab.

'It's going to be OK,' he said.

I'm beginning to think that maybe, just maybe he was right.

ACKNOWLEDGEMENTS

Thank you to my agent Emily, for her unwavering support and being my first 'yes' in a long time. David Headley for his unshakable calm and support. To my brilliant and patient editor Ciara Lloyd for believing in my story, and in my writing. To all the team at Blink Publishing – you really are the dream team. Thank you for taking a bet on me and all your hard work. Pete Selby, for his initial belief and vision, James Lilford, all my Curtis Brown creative crew, Sarah Hiscox for being a wonderful support and friend. Lou, Eric, Sylvia, Ying, James. Pink Camel crew, Carmel and all my Recovery pals. Andrew, Rachael and all my Manchester day ones, Christie Watson for being the best tutor and cheerleader in the early days. Butter – thanks for loving me and making me laugh. To my family – I'm sorry if I overshared a bit in these pages, and hope you got to the end and understood why I had to be so honest. I love you.

To the ones no longer here – thanks for hearing my

prayers and keep giving me those signs when I least expect, but always need them the most

Finally to the reader. Thanks for making it to the end of this book. I am truly grateful.